CHARLES HADDON SPURGEON.

Yours heartily

C.H. Spurgeon

CHARLES HADDON SPURGEON

Preacher, Author, and Philanthropist.

WITH ANECDOTAL REMINISCENCES

BY

G. HOLDEN PIKE
AUTHOR OF "THE ROMANCE OF PIETISM," ETC.

TORONTO:
S. R. BRIGGS,
TORONTO WILLARD TRACT DEPOSITORY AND
BIBLE DEPOT,
CORNER OF YONGE AND TEMPERANCE STREETS.

Engraved by J.Cochran from a Photograph

CHARLES HADDON SPURGEON:

Preacher, Author, and Philanthropist.

WITH ANECDOTAL REMINISCENCES.

BY

G. HOLDEN PIKE,

AUTHOR OF "THE ROMANCE OF THE STREETS," ETC.

TORONTO:

S. R. BRIGGS,

TORONTO WILLARD TRACT DEPOSITORY AND
BIBLE DEPÔT,
CORNER OF YONGE AND TEMPERANCE STREETS.

Printed by Hazell, Watson, & Viney, Ld., London and Aylesbury.

PREFACE.

I HAVE endeavoured in this volume to tell
the public what I thought they would like
to know respecting Mr. Spurgeon and his work
without unduly prying into the Pastor's private
life.

Ten years ago I published, through Messrs.
James Clarke & Co., a *brochure* on this same
subject, which found some acceptance ; and with
my friends' permission I have reprinted a few
pages from that little work, much of which is now
out of date.

In 1878 I also issued, through Messrs. Passmore & Alabaster, " Seven Portraits, etc., with
Reminiscences of Life at Waterbeach and London."
I have also given some passages from that
pamphlet, the main attraction of which, however,

consists in the admirably executed frontispiece, which gives Mr. Spurgeon's portrait at seven different periods of his career.

With the exceptions named, I have drawn my materials from all available sources; and I have done my best to avoid errors, and all things beside which could in any way occasion annoyance· My one aim has been to please Mr. Spurgeon's wide circle of friends, and to advance the common cause in which the Pastor is engaged.

G. H. P.

London, *October* 1886.

CONTENTS.

CHAPTER I.

CHAPTER VIII.

CHAPTER IX.

CHAPTER X.

CHAPTER XI.

MR. SPURGEON'S EARLY DAYS.

"I will ask any sensible man, above all, any serious Christian here, whether there have not been certain times in his life when he could most distinctly see that indeed God did 'choose his inheritance for him'? . . . I do not know whether all of you can go with me here; but I think you must in some instance or other be forced to see, that God has indeed ordained your inheritance for you. If you cannot, I can. I can see a thousand chances, as men would call them, all working together like wheels in a great piece of machinery, to fix me just where I am; and I can look back to a hundred places where, if one of those little wheels had run away—if one of those little atoms in the great whirlpool of my existence had started aside—I might have been anywhere but here, occupying a very different position. If you cannot say this, I know *I* can with emphasis, and can trace God's hand back to the period of my birth through every step I have taken; I can feel that indeed God has allotted my inheritance for me. If any of you are so wilfully beclouded that you will not see the hand of God in your being, and will insist that all has been done by your will without Providence; that you have been left to steer your own course across the ocean of existence; and that you are where you are because your own hand guided the tiller, and your own arm directed the rudder, all I can say is, my own experience belies the fact, and the experience of many now in this place would rise in testimony against you, and say, 'Verily, it is not in man that walketh to direct his steps.' —'Man proposes, but God disposes;' and the God of heaven is not unoccupied, but is engaged in over-ruling, ordering, altering, working all things according to the good pleasure of His will."—*The New Park Street Pulpit*, i. 255.

I.

MR. SPURGEON'S EARLY DAYS.

MANY hands have tried to do what I shall certainly not attempt in this volume—to write the life of Mr. Spurgeon. To accomplish such a task would be as impossible to-day as it will be in the future. No great man can be worthily preserved on paper—not even by the most perfect Boswellian mode of treatment; and what the Pastor has been heard to threaten he will do, should he ever be approached by a first cousin of Johnson's biographer, may well intimidate the boldest member of that inquisitive tribe. I am not a Boswell; I am not a biographer. I shall not impertinently pry behind the scenes of private life to annoy a worthy family on the one hand, and to gratify a morbid public curiosity on the other hand. All that is purposed to be done is, to produce a series of sketches different from anything which has, as yet, been put together in a volume, and which shall be sufficiently true to life not to mislead outsiders, and not to shock the sensibilities of friends.

In case any reader should need them for reference, I shall, in this opening chapter, put down a few commonplace facts such as are widely known and are everybody's property. Mr. Spurgeon was born at Kelvedon, in Essex, on the 19th of June, 1834 ; and, as the world is fond of comparing the events in the life of one great man with those belonging to the course of another great man, it may be remarked that on that auspicious day Thomas Babington Macaulay "crossed the frontier of Mysore." It was in that year, moreover, that the Houses of Parliament were destroyed by fire.

During several generations, the Spurgeons have been engaged in the Christian ministry. The Pastor's grandfather spent half a century among a flock at Stambourne, and this old worthy's son is a valued minister of the Independent denomination at the present time. One of the earliest custodians of the popular preacher was an affectionate maiden aunt, who, with others, could not fail to detect a precocious talent in her youthful charge. We have all heard how Richard Knill looked upon the boy with admiration, to express hopes in regard to the future which have not been disappointed.

Some years ago the Rev. W. Osborne, who is now pastor of a flourishing Baptist Church at Eastbourne, supplied me with the following reminiscence of the Rev. James Spurgeon of Stambourne :—

The day preceding that on which he entered on college work in London, Mr. Osborne preached at Stambourne for old Mr. Spurgeon, who was then an octogenarian, and showed the strongest possible partiality for Dr. Watts's hymns. This deep-rooted prejudice on the part of the old gentleman was a trait in his character with which the neighbours and regular hearers were familiar ; but it was something of which the young preacher had never heard even the slightest whisper. Mr. Osborne arrived at Stambourne, he entered the chapel, to receive the first intimation of a coming disagreement when a member of the congregation expressed a hope that the hymns were selected, and that all were of Dr. Watts's composition. On turning to the book it was at once seen that the unlucky youth had missed his way in each selection, every hymn being the production of an unappreciated poet, for none would suit the old gentleman but those of Isaac Watts. Time was pressing, however, and the hymns were allowed to pass ; but as the service went on, the effects of the strange verses on the mind of the old pastor

were striking, and calculated to create trepidation
in the heart of an inexperienced preacher. Like
a master in Israel the old man took a seat in the
table-pew, and, as occasion required, he cast a
searching glance towards the pulpit. When the
first hymn was announced he signified his dis-
approval by gravely shaking his head ; when the
second was given out, with no improvement, he
expressed his disgust by simply closing the book ;
but when the third came, and was still by a for-
bidden author, he raised his fist as though he
would chastise the offender. At the conclusion of
the service there was an explosion, not of wrath,
but of pent-up feeling. " Young man ! " cried the
aged pastor, with a genial twinkle of the eye,
while he raised a stout stick to give emphasis to
his words—" Young man ! if you do not want
your brains knocked out, you *must* sing Dr.
Watts's hymns ! " If he was not actually terrified
into compliance with these forcible demands,
Mr. Osborne took particular care not to repeat in
the afternoon the mistake of the morning. At
this second service hymns by Dr. Watts were
quietly introduced ; old Mr. Spurgeon according
the preacher a nod of approval as soon as the
first was announced. When the second and
third hymns were such as could be commended,
former chagrin gave place to extreme satisfaction.

' ' Right, sir, right ! " cried the pastor, after listening admiringly to a sermon on the fall of Jericho, " I am glad to see you can appreciate the best authors so quickly. Go now and get your ram's horn ready, like those men, and God may make you the means of hurling to the ground walls as strong and stubborn as those "—*i.e.*, of Jericho. On the following day Mr. Osborne removed to London, joined the Pastors' College, and thus got his " ram's horn ready " for future service in a manner that won the approval of his honest, outspoken preceptor.

It is generally understood that Mr. Spurgeon showed his ministerial proclivities almost as soon as he could walk and speak. His earliest recollections are of reading religious books ; and in childish days he would address an audience, corresponding in age to his own years, with more force than some adults can command in the pulpit. Very strong tendencies in a certain direction in childhood are always interesting ; they must have been doubly so in a case where the subject was endowed with one of the finest voices of which we have any example. Though thus piously brought up, he was not converted until. he was sixteen, and the great change occurred at Colchester, in which town he purposed to visit one sanctuary after another in search of saving light. He turned into one of the humblest of chapels, and there heard a thin, pale man preach from the words, "Look unto Me and be ye saved, all the ends of the earth." The manner in which the preacher cried, "Look! *Look!* LOOK!" was peculiarly striking, and, what is better, relief came instantly, the simplicity of the Gospel being at once appreciated. The pulpit in which this memorable "Look" sermon was preached may now be seen at the Stockwell Orphanage.

On a certain occasion, Mr. Spurgeon's father, in speaking of his family to Dr. Ford, of America, is reported to have remarked :—"I had been from home a great deal, trying to build up weak congregations, and felt that I was neglecting the religious training of my own children while I toiled for the good of others. I returned home with these feelings. I opened the door, and was surprised to find none of the children about the hall. Going quietly up the stairs, I heard my wife's voice. She was engaged in prayer with the children. I heard her pray for them one by one by name. She came to Charles, and specially prayed for him, for he was of high spirit and daring temper. I listened till she had ended her prayer, and I felt and said, 'Lord, I will go on with Thy work. The children will be cared for.'"

Of his education after this date, little needs to be said. He plodded as a schoolboy at Colchester. He studied for a time at Maidstone, in an agricultural college of that town. He subsequently accepted an appointment in a school at Newmarket, the principal of which was a Baptist ; but I am not aware that this fact in any way accounts for the change of sentiment— the transition from Pædobaptist to Baptist views —which about this time occurred. That change was brought about by a close study of the Bible ; for Mr. Spurgeon's mind is of an independent cast, that would not brook the interference of any lower authority than Scripture. Thus early his mind was active, while his industry was great. A slight *brochure* of those days, called "Antichrist and her Brood," has never been published, although I believe that the MS. is still in the possession of the Rev. John Spurgeon. A poem called "The Fall of Jericho" was printed, and afterwards republished in the first number of *The Sword and the Trowel.*

Before his conversion, and as a mere youth, Mr. Spurgeon was tempted to become an unbeliever ; and while preaching at Exeter Hall, on Sunday evening, March 18th, 1855, he gave some vivid reminiscences of that unhappy time

e.g.—" There may be some one here to-night who
has come without faith, a man of reason, a free-
thinker.   With him I have no argument at all.
I profess not to stand here as a controversialist,
but as a preacher of things that I know and feel.
But I too have been like him.   There was an
evil hour when once I slipped the anchor of my
faith ; I cut the cable of my belief ; I no longer
moored myself hard by the coasts of revelation ;
I allowed my vessel to drift before the wind ; I
said to reason, 'Be thou my captain ;' I said
to my own brain, 'Be thou my rudder ;' and I
started on my mad voyage.   Thank God it is
all over now ; but I will tell you its brief history.
It was one hurried sailing over the tempestuous
ocean of free thought.   I went on, and as I
went the skies began to darken ; but to make
up for that deficiency the waters were brilliant
with coruscations of brilliancy.   I saw sparks
flying upwards that pleased me, and I thought,
' If this be free thought, it is a happy thing.'
My thoughts seemed gems, and I scattered stars
with both my hands.   But anon, instead of these
coruscations of glory, I saw grim fiends, fierce
and horrible, start up from the waters, and as I
dashed on they gnashed their teeth and grinned
upon me ; they seized the prow of my ship and
dragged me on, while I, in part, gloried at the

rapidity of my motion, but yet shuddered at the terrific rate with which I passed the old landmarks of my faith. As I hurried forward with an awful speed, I began to doubt my very existence ; I doubted if there were a world, I doubted if there were such a thing as myself. I went to the very verge of the dreary realms of unbelief. I went to the very bottom of the sea of infidelity. I doubted everything. But here the devil foiled himself ; for the very extravagance of the doubt proved its absurdity. Just when I saw the bottom of that sea, there came a voice which said, 'And can this doubt be true ?' At this very thought I awoke. I started from that death-dream, which God knows might have damned my soul, and ruined this my body, if I had not awoke. When I arose faith took the helm ; from that moment I doubted not. Faith steered me back ; faith cried, 'Away, away!' I cast my anchor on Calvary ; I lifted my eye to God ; and here I am alive, and out of hell. Therefore, I speak what I do know. I have sailed that perilous voyage ; I have come safe to land. Ask me again to be an infidel ! No ; I have tried it ; it was sweet at first, but bitter afterwards."

I will now briefly allude to the pastor's first sermon, and then return to some other things

which were providentially overruled to produce
the best results in after days.

On a certain day, between twenty and thirty
years ago, two young men might have been seen
walking out of Cambridge towards a village lying
in the suburbs of that town, for the purpose of
holding a cottage service. Neither of the two
pedestrians had ever preached a sermon in his
life ; but more singular was the fact that each
marched forward along the green level lanes
while harbouring the comfortable mistake that
the other was the preacher for the day. They
talked as they travelled, and, after a time, the
younger ventured to intimate to his companion
that he hoped the Lord would bless his—the
companion's—labours. Those words as they fell
appear to have produced something akin to an
electric shock. "Oh, dear !" cried the elder
youth, eagerly, desirous of correcting an inconvenient error—"Oh, dear, I never preached in my
life. I never thought of doing such a thing. I
was asked to walk with you, and I sincerely hope
God will bless *you* in *your* preaching." "Nay,"
cried the younger, apparently growing nervous,
"but I never preached, and I don't know that
I could do anything of the sort." The elder
had thrown off the burden ; the younger walked
on, filled with fear and trembling. There was

the cottage, there were the people assembled, and a sermon would have to be preached to them. The effort was made ; the younger of the two novices made that effort, succeeded beyond his expectations—and his name was Charles Haddon Spurgeon.

For years before this eventful day in his history he had shown himself to be of a strongly inquisitive mind. Having once set his heart on knowing a thing, he would persevere until he came at the truth, nor would he allow his reasonable curiosity to be evaded either by the friendly " Pooh, pooh ! " or by sterner rebuke. In an autobiographical article, published more than ten years ago, we are supplied with some juvenile reminiscences far too characteristic to be overlooked. When as a child he was living with his grandfather, it was the custom for Charles Haddon to read the Scriptures at family worship, and on every occasion he was allowed the licence of asking any question he chose on the portion for the day. On a certain morning the inconveniently-inquisitive reader came to the " bottomless pit " of the Revelation, and immediately asked, " Grandpa, what can this mean ? " " Pooh, pooh ! child, go on," replied the old man, regarding the question as too trivial to call for serious reply. To a child, however, every subject of interest is important; and in this instance Charles determined to read the same chapter morning after morning until a satisfactory explanation should be offered. "Well, dear, what is it that puzzles you?" asked the grandfather, after he had heard about the Beast, the Mother of Harlots, etc., etc., etc., as often as he thought desirable, or perhaps profitable. The question was then put in a more definite form, "If the pit aforesaid had no bottom, where would all those people fall to who dropped out at its lower end?" The query was too deep to be answered at once; it seems to have disturbed the gravity of the little circle, and to have been a sample of the "difficulties" that were propounded for elucidation at family worship.

The late sainted Mr. Knill, of Chester, was a friend of the family in those early days, and he happened to be drawn in an extraordinary manner towards the child whose singularities were sufficiently marked to make him an object of more than ordinary interest. One fine morning Mr. Knill awoke his *protégé* at an early hour, and for some time they walked together in the garden. They conversed about books and reading, and about the privilege of winning souls for Christ. Then they knelt together in the arbour, where the elder prayed for the younger, and did so in a manner that brought a blessing and left a life-long impression. Afterwards, in the midst of the family circle, Mr. Knill placed the child on his knee, and remarked, "I do not know how it is, but I feel a solemn presentiment this child will preach the Gospel to thousands, and God will bless him to many souls. So sure am I of this, that when my little man preaches in Rowland Hill's Chapel—as he will do one day—I should like him to promise me that he will give out the hymn beginning

> "'God moves in a mysterious way
> His wonders to perform.'"

That rather striking prophecy was completely fulfilled ; but Mr. Spurgeon is of opinion that the words themselves were instrumental in bringing about their own fulfilment.

The "first sermon" has been already mentioned. When the ice was once broken, the neighbourhood of Cambridge was the scene of the young Christian's evangelistic efforts. On arriving at a village on an unpropitious wintry night he has found the chapel empty, and has, lantern in hand, gone round to the houses to collect a congregation. It is quite a mistake to suppose that he was not popular before coming to London ; for he was a favourite with the Cambridgeshire peasantry before he became so conspicuous a

figure in the outer world and the leading member
of his denomination.   When stationed at Waterbeach, his services began to be in excessive
demand, and invitations to preach were cordially
responded to.   The more shrewd even among the
common people must have perceived that one who
was something more than a rising man was in
their midst.

In youth he did not altogether set his face
against going to college, though in later life he
has " a thousand times thanked the Lord very
heartily for the strange providence which forced
his steps into another and far better path."
Truth to say, Mr. Spurgeon missed a collegiate
training consequent on one of those singular
mishaps which, at the time, are as annoying as
they are unavoidable.   While he was carrying
all before him at Waterbeach his judicious seniors
thought that the pastor would never become all
he was capable of becoming unless he went to
London and sat the prescribed number of times
at the feet of a duly-qualified professor.   This
advice was listened to, and arrangements were
made for a meeting of Dr. Angus on the one
part and Mr. Spurgeon on the other part, the
rendezvous appointed having been the house
of the well-known publisher, Mr. Macmillan, of
Cambridge.   The young pastor arrived at the

time specified, was ushered into a drawing-room
by the maid, and, after waiting for two hours,
he rang the bell to learn the reason of the protracted delay. In the meantime, Dr. Angus had
arrived, had been shown into another room, but
not being so well able to exemplify the virtue
of patience as his younger friend, the learned
doctor departed for London, doubtless wondering
why young aspirants to the ministry were not
more eager to seize fleeting opportunities. Thus
the two sat in adjoining rooms until patience
had " had her perfect work," neither suspecting
that the other was near. What momentous consequences sometimes hang on small matters ! how
much may occasionally depend on the remissness
of a half-witted servant-maid ! Still, the Church
would have gained nothing by C. H. Spurgeon's
admission into Regent's Park College.

Writing in 1881, Mr. Spurgeon thus referred
to his own days of early plodding :—

" My college course was after this fashion. I
was for three years a Cambridge man, though I
never entered the University. I could not have
obtained a degree, because I was a Nonconformist ; and, moreover, it was a better thing for
me to pursue my studies under an admirable
scholar and tender friend, and preach at the same
time. I must have been a singular-looking youth

2

on wet evenings. During the last year of my stay in Cambridge, when I had given up my office as usher, I was wont to sally forth every night in the week except Saturday, and walk three, five, or perhaps eight miles out and back again on my preaching work ; and when it rained I dressed myself in waterproof leggings and a mackintosh coat, and a hat with a waterproof covering, and I carried a dark lantern to show me the way across the fields. I had many adventures . . . but what I had gathered by my studies during the day I handed out to a company of villagers in the evening, and was greatly profited by the exercise. I always found it good to say my lesson when I had learned it. Children do so, and it is equally good for preachers, especially if they say their lesson by heart. In my young days I fear I said many odd things and made many blunders, but my audiences were not hypercritical, and no newspaper writers dogged my heels ; and so I had a happy training-ground in which, by continual practice, I attained such a degree of ready speech as I now possess. There is no way of learning to preach which can be compared to preaching itself. If you want to swim you must get into the water, and if you at the first make a sorry exhibition, never mind, for it is by swimming as you can that you learn to swim as you should.   Hence we ought to be lenient with beginners, for they will do better by-and-bye.   If young speakers in Cambridge had been discouraged and silenced, I might not have found my way here, and, therefore, I hope I shall be the last to bring forth a wet blanket for any who sincerely speak for Christ, however humble may be their endeavours.   The fear of there being too many preachers is the last that will occur to me.   I rejoice in that passage of the psalm, 'The Lord gave the word ; great was the company of those that published it.'   Go forth, young man, and proclaim among the people of this vast city all the words of this life.   Among these millions you will all be few enough. . . . Fill your baskets with living seed, and in due season bring them back laden with many sheaves.   My heart is with you ; my soul rejoices in your successes ; and I look to the great Head of the Church, through your means, to gather in His blood-bought ones."

Speaking at the laying of the first stone of the Metropolitan Tabernacle, August 16th, 1859, the Rev. John Spurgeon thus referred to his son's early days :—

" I always thought my son did wrong in coming to London ; now you see that I was wrong.   I always thought he was wrong in not going to

college ; I tried three or four hours with him one
night with a dear friend that loved him, but it
was no use ; he said, 'No, I will never go to
college, only in strict obedience to you as a
father.' There I left the matter ; and I see that
God has been with him, though I thought it was
a wrong step in him to go to London. And I
thought it was a wrong step for me to come here
to-night ; but perhaps I may be mistaken again.
I can tell you it is one of the happiest days of
my life. I feel beyond myself when I think of
the kindness that has been shown to him when
but a youth. I ascribe it all to God's goodness
and the earnest prayers of his people. He has
been exposed to temptation from every source,
and even now, my friends, he is not free from it.
You have prayed for him, and God has sustained
him. Oh! let me entreat you to continue your
prayers. Every one here to-night, go home and
pray for your pastor. A meeting like this is
enough to carry a man beyond himself and fill
his heart with pride ; but the grace of God is
all-sufficient. Several persons said to me—I do
not know what their motive was—'Your son will
never last in London six months ; he has no
education.' I said, 'You are terribly mistaken ;
he has the best education that can possibly be
had ; God has been his teacher, and he has had

earthly teachers too.' I knew, as far as education
went, he could manage London very well. Then
they said his health would fail ; but it has not
failed him yet. He has had enough to shake
his constitution, it is true, but God has been very
merciful to him. I think if there is one thing
that would crown my happiness to-day, it would
have been to see his grandfather here. I should
have loved to see him here. He said, 'Boy, don't
ask me to go, I am too old ; I am overcome with
God's goodness and mercy to me.' He is always
talking about him. Old people like to have
something to talk about, 'so he always talks about
his grandson. And next to that I should like,
my dear friends, to have seen his mother here.
I believe, under God's grace, his mother has been
the means of leading him to Christ. You are
well aware that I go and talk in the best manner
I can to a few poor people on the Sabbath day,
and God has blessed my labours. I thought,
however, I ought not to go out on the Sabbath
day, as God's people should train up their children
in the best way they can ; I thought I was neglecting my children, and as I came home one
evening about seven o'clock, and went upstairs,
I heard the voice of a mother pleading for her
boy Charles, and talking to him and the others,
and pouring her heart out in prayer in such a

way as I never did in my life, and as I never
heard before. It is for the encouragement of
mothers that I mention this, that you may pray
for your children, for God is a prayer-hearing
and prayer-answering God."

Whilst taking a retrospect of a third of a
century of work, we become conscious of feeling
unwontedly curious about the youthful associations of one whom we may pronounce to be the
first preacher of this age without fear of contra-
diction. What signs of unusual genius, of future
distinction, were visible during youth? Who
were his friends? where may we trace the foot-
prints of his first travels as a preacher? Feeling
more than ordinary interest in these minutiæ, I
some years ago asked a friend, whose fortune it
was to reside near " Ouse's silent tide," if he
would collect such *ana* as he could relating to
Mr. Spurgeon's early days in that vicinity.

I believe there are about a score of Houghtons
in the British Empire; but to myself the one
interesting member of a numerous family is that
Houghton which lies low and snug among the
tall trees luxuriating on the banks of the broad,
slow-rolling Ouse, midway between Huntingdon
and St. Ives. It is not a spot whereon one
would at first expect to find any religious
memories of more than common interest; but

in this case appearances are, happily, deceptive.
Near Houghton, Dr. Brooke, an able preacher,
and father of the well-known Rev. Stopford
Brooke, was for some time stationed. Here also
laboured Mr. Edward Cressell, a minister of the
Independent denomination, and whose ministra-
tions were heartily appreciated by the homely
village folk of the neighbourhood, and by lovers
of good preaching farther away. Above all, it
was at Houghton in his early days that Mr.
Spurgeon became the guest of the eccentric Potto
Brown, called by Elihu Burritt, in one of his
books, "The Miller of Houghton." Mr. Brown
was thoroughly eccentric, but he was still a kind-
hearted man, who grew hot-house grapes for the
sick poor, and who could commend the Wes-
leyans for saving souls at a cheaper rate than
was done by any other denomination. On this
question, as well as on others, the youth and
the veteran were far from being agreed, and
consequently some lively discussions came off
between the two which for smartness would not
have disgraced the Literary Club in its palmiest
days.

I will now give what my Ouse-side friend
says about Houghton, its famous miller, and the
youthful preacher, C. H. Spurgeon :—

"It has been with much interest that I have

traced, by the aid of the memories of my acquaintances, the early teachings and appearance of one who has taken and maintained an honoured place in the vineyard of Jesus Christ, and one who has well borne the burden and heat of the day. A gentleman, whom I took to be a relative, informed me that he heard Mr. Spurgeon preach his first sermon when about fourteen years of age, and he then read, prayed, and expounded the Word, being attired in a round jacket and broad, turn-down collar, such as I remember to have seen in fashion at that period.

"Mr. C. D. tells me that he remembers C. H. Spurgeon preaching at Somersham about twenty-six years ago, and when he would be about seventeen years of age. He was then wearing a round jacket and turn-down collar. He remembers the words of the text, though not their place—'Fear not, thou worm Jacob.' The boyish voice of the preacher afforded a striking and impressive contrast to the tones of the aged minister who was accustomed to occupy the pulpit.

"Mr. Spurgeon was then living at some place near Cambridge, and his mode of preaching afforded promise that he would become a powerful and popular speaker. One old man, who was a Particular Baptist, and, I believe, difficult to please, went to hear him, and was careful to repeat the visit.

"One old minister, for whom Mr. Spurgeon preached, was plagued with a bad wife, and she must needs go to America; but with great patience the husband waited for her return, never fastening the door of the house nor suffering others to do so till she came back to him.

"Mrs. J. A. remembers Mr. Spurgeon preaching at Houghton when quite a lad. She remembers the sermon was a very impressive one, and could it have been heard without seeing the boyish preacher, any one would have taken it to be the discourse of a staid and experienced Christian. She believes this was one thing that led Mr. Potto Brown to look upon the youthful orator with less favour than he might otherwise have done, because he thought that the sermon could not have been his own composition.

"Mrs. B. appears to me to have a more vivid recollection of the impression of what Mrs. J. A. felt at the time above stated. There was much conversation between the youthful preacher and Mr. Potto Brown, and evidently much contention, too; for each would hold firmly to his own opinion.

"Mrs. C. tells me that her husband, who was the schoolmaster at the time, was struck by the precocious talent of the young preacher, and with his general style of preaching."

The above notes were collected for me by the late Edward Cressell, whose friendship I highly valued, and who, as pastor of the Congregational Church, Houghton, Hunts, was one of the best preachers in the neighbourhood. The information is now, I believe, regarded as common property by *quidnuncs* in both the Old and the New World.

In regard to Mr. Spurgeon and the late Potto Brown, the Pastor on one occasion himself referred to that memorable meeting—" How he shocked our Calvinistic propriety ! . . . We recollect his telling us that our preaching was *very well for an apprentice boy*, which was no doubt a correct estimate, but after he had spoken in that style one felt quite at home with him, and gave him a Roland for his Oliver without the slightest compunction. It was a battle royal, and both the old gentleman and the 'prentice boy grew sufficiently warm ; but no scars remained on either combatant. Mr. Brown walked with us to Huntingdon in loving conversation, and afterwards sent us Haldane's *Life* as a present."

REMINISCENCES OF WATERBEACH.

I. THE VILLAGE AND ITS SURROUNDINGS.

II. RECOLLECTIONS OF MR. SPURGEON'S PASTORATE.

"When I think upon the all but infinite mischief which may result from a mistake as to our vocation for the Christian pastorate, I feel overwhelmed with fear lest any of us should be slack in examining our credentials; and I had rather that we stood too much in doubt, and examined too frequently, than that we should become cumberers of the ground. There are not lacking many exact methods by which a man may test his call to the ministry if he earnestly desires to do so. It is imperative upon him not to enter the ministry until he has made solemn quest and trial of himself as to this point. His own personal salvation being secure, he must investigate as to the further matter of his call to office; the first is vital to himself as a Christian, the second equally vital to him as a pastor. As well be a professor without conversion, as a pastor without calling. In both cases there is a name and nothing more."—*Lectures to My Students*, i. 23.

II.

I.—THE VILLAGE AND ITS SURROUNDINGS.

AS the village in which Mr. Spurgeon commenced his pastoral career, Waterbeach seemed to be worthy of a special visit, so that when the opportunity occurred I undertook the journey. The parish lies about five miles north of Cambridge, the soil is remarkably rich, and on leaving the station the tourist will not fail to observe the tokens of more than average prosperity everywhere manifest ; while the magnificent dome of sky presents that aspect of immensity which is particularly noticeable on great level areas such as the Cambridgeshire flats and the neighbouring fens. At the last census the population had been put down at sixteen hundred and nineteen, and one might despair of finding a more comfortable agricultural settlement. The inhabitants eat the fruits of their luxuriant marshes while sitting beneath their own vines and

fig trees; for, instead of belonging to one
domineering autocrat, the land is divided into
small proprietorships. The people are, consequently, as remarkable for their independence in
religious matters as they are for their Liberalism
in politics. They are an honest, hospitable folk,
always ready to entertain a stranger, and while
characterised by hereditary prejudices, know only
of two hemispheres—Waterbeach and Mark Lane.
Their prejudices are going one by one. The open
sewer, for example, which formerly crossed and
fumigated the village, has been covered over,
though the older " Conservatives " battled bravely
on behalf of a venerable institution; and a
smithy, black and begrimed, still defiling the
middle of the " Green," was said to be already
doomed. Nonconformity was everywhere in the
ascendant, and the vicar, who was a decided
Evangelical, appeared to lead the pleasantest
existence possible by simply preaching the Gospel
instead of fighting the sects. Were his procedure
less judicious he would wage unequal war, and
would, besides, risk changing present friends into
ecclesiastical wasps. Fully to realise the anomaly,
remember that we were just ten minutes' ride
from the University, and that though Waterbeach
Church attracted one of the best congregations in
the vicinity, yet the parish, as I understood, con-

tained only one large farmer, and a few small
ones, who were Churchmen ; and then commend
a vicar who, under such conditions, could command
the loving esteem of every parishioner.

Such being the character of Waterbeach, we
cannot wonder that in his youth Mr. Spurgeon
found the village to be a congenial sphere, that
he did his share in confirming the Puritan-like
faith and politics of the people, while his own
character may have taken a colouring from his
associations. In a strain which a certain critic
judges to be worthy of "The Complete Letter
Writer," he referred to his charge, at the age
of nineteen, as a "little Garden of Eden," and
only poverty obliged him to sever the tie of
union. Had Mr. Spurgeon's ministry commenced
in these times, instead of at the date it did,
Waterbeach would, undoubtedly, have held its
own a year or two longer, in spite of the call
to London. The people are immensely proud
of their old connection ; and still, in a manner,
regarding their late pastor as one of themselves,
always welcome him back into their midst with
fervent enthusiasm. This regard would appear
to be pretty general among high and low.
At the best tables no guest would be allowed
to speak words of detraction unchallenged ; and
no one, who is nice as regards consequences,

would impugn Spurgeon's orthodoxy or good nature among the peasants at any one of the village lounges.

After alighting from the train, I had scarce advanced a hundred yards towards the village when it was my good fortune to encounter Mr. James Toller, of Winfold Farm. Mr. Toller is a pillar of the Nonconformist interest in Waterbeach, he is a liberal contributor to the institutions at the Metropolitan Tabernacle, and Mr. Spurgeon himself has, more than once, been a guest at the worthy yeoman's house. One piece of luck—the word is used by the compilers of the Prayer-Book—was soon followed by another; for the clouds, which had threatened rain, broke and lightened, so that we were even privileged to see Waterbeach in the autumn sunshine.

After paying our respects at the manse of the Baptist pastor, and looking in at the village news-room, we find ourselves on that eminently interesting site—the scene of Mr. Spurgeon's first pastorate. The old thatched chapel has, however, disappeared—we feel a sort of selfish regret that it should be so—it has given place to a handsome and more commodious meeting-house, the corner-stones of which were respectively laid by Mr. Spurgeon and Mr. Toller.

Still, the site is the same, and that is enough for
our present purpose. On this very ground, a
generation ago, many honest country folk
assembled for worship who already began to
wonder whereunto the thing would grow. The
then boy-preacher not only edified and surprised
the people who crowded the little chapel; there
were some hearers there who, though poor and
unlettered, were yet sufficiently discerning to
know that an uncommon genius was in their
midst. " He astonished everybody at that time ? "
I inquired of an elderly deacon who well remembers every circumstance. " Of course he did ! "
was the quick, curt reply. " How, then, did he
preach ? " " Why," continued the old man, looking straight at me, as though I ought to know
all about it, " like a man a hundred years old
in experience ! " That honest deacon afterwards
visited London for the first time ; he went the
countryman's usual round of inspection in the
capital, saw the Metropolitan Tabernacle, and
sat down as a guest of the pastor in his house
at Clapham. On his return he tried to tell the
people what he had really seen ; but memory
grew confused. His unsophisticated mind seemed
to retain but one thing, the lustre of which
darkened everything else—" Mr. Spurgeon was
very glad to see me."

Winfold Farm covers an area of nearly six hundred acres, and the residence is a mile from the village. The proprietor of this fertile inheritance is Mr. Toller's eldest son, a young gentleman who had then just come of age, and who resided with his father. In the opinion of Mr. Toller no man can be a landlord and tenant at the same time, and earn a competence—the shortest road to bankruptcy is over your own land as a gentleman farmer. There is more philosophy in this reasoning than a townsman can gainsay.

The admirer of fine breeds will find enough of entertainment at Winfold Farm ; and by a little judicious selection from the bullocks in the straw-yard, and the sheep in the turnip-field, a very taking cattle-show might be put together —especially if the thing were supplemented with a few choice pigs, and with some more than admirable specimens of horse-flesh which would be available. But more akin to our subject is the acre of land which is annually set apart for the orphans of Stockwell, the produce of flour and potatoes being despatched to London every autumn. The best things on the estate are not deemed too good to bestow freely upon Mr. Spurgeon's Institutions ; to be but a friend of the pastor is to carry a passport to liberal entertainment. Only a day or two before, a well-known gentleman, then in repute at the Metropolitan Tabernacle, had been down to Winfold for the purpose of enjoying "a little sport." Provided with the most perfect of breech-loaders, he started forth to bang and blaze away his powder at a prodigal rate, though from morn to dusk he did not even ruffle the feathers of a single native bird. Any stray rambler at whom this amateur might have directly aimed would have risked no bodily harm, the general opinion, as Mr. Toller explained, being that the marksman would not have hit the house had he levelled and fired with that intention. But still, ramblers abroad were seriously threatened by the stray shots which, for the time, whizzed hither and thither in wild irregularity. Such is the account Mr. Toller gave of his sporting guest, who, it scarce need be said, was not that ready marksman—but not with firearms—Mr. Spurgeon himself.

A walk before dinner being proposed, Mr. Toller conducted my companion and myself to Denney Abbey Farm, the estate adjoining his own, the dwelling-house and outbuildings being the remains of a pre-Reformation monastery, of which Mr. Richard Toller was found to be the master. Everything here is weird and antiquated to a degree which is sufficiently pleasing on a summer day, when the objects of interest can be seen and enjoyed ; but the effect is less pleasing when the shades of night are falling, and the winter wind, moaning around the tall, stout chimneys, seems to be Old Nature's funeral requiem over monks and nuns whose bones are thickly packed beneath the garden soil.   It is as strange as true that owls, bats, and other night-birds find at Denney a congenial retreat wherein to screech and croak away the midnight hour.   When the business of the day is hushed, one might easily associate the clanking of a horse's halter chain with the creaking of a Templar's armour, as he would once have ridden from the courtyard to join the First Crusade ; or the pattering of a cat's feet on the garden-walk might remind one of those light-treading maidens whose lives were consecrated to God and St. Clare.   But as we are not superstitious, and the sun is shining, let us deal with sober fact.

In the year 1160, Robert Chamberlain, Earl of Richmond, became a monk at Ely, some ten miles distant, and being a man of enterprising piety, he gave an island in the surrounding mere for holy purposes.   A cell for a few hardy brethren was accordingly erected ; but when repeated floods obliged them to remove they encamped on higher ground, bestowed by Aubrey Picot, at Denney.

After they had held the site for a few years, the Ely monks were superseded by those daring foes of Moslem infidels, the Knights Templars, to whose wealthy Order the manor of Waterbeach belonged. In the fourteenth century the society of Templars was abolished, when their forsaken cells were occupied by the nuns of St. Clare, twenty-five of whom resided here on an income of £172 a-year. After the dissolution of the religious houses, at the era of the Reformation, Denney passed from one owner to another; and in the reign of Elizabeth the farm was rented, I believe, by Hobson, the carrier of Cambridge, the first master who let out hired horses, and in whose stables the familiar proverb "Hobson's choice" is known to have originated. It is not probable that the property has undergone any great changes during the last century. The dwelling-house is a portion of the original Church, founded in 1160, and rebuilt by the Countess of Pembroke in the reign of Edward III. Some of the outbuildings appear to have been removed, or to have gradually fallen into decay, though for several generations the ancient refectory has served as a convenient barn. When the convent was in its prime a double entrenchment encircled its towers, and instead of traversing the country on foot, or by horse, as in after years, the monks plied their oars across the mere, which then spread its broad smooth surface between Denney and Ely.

We now return to Winfold to dine and to rest away the afternoon. When at last we finally take leave of our friends, we are conscious of having been entertained in a worthy Old English style, and also of having spent an agreeable holiday, on ground which will still be visited by summer tourists for its own sake, and also on account of its happy association with the first pastorate of Charles Haddon Spurgeon.

II.—Recollections of Mr. Spurgeon's Pastorate.

Some time after the adventure just related I determined on paying a second visit to the scene of Mr. Spurgeon's first pastorate.

It had been a wet night, and the damp, cold November morning was but the prelude to a soaking, tempestuous day, the wind and the rain having completed an alliance which was destined to hold good through another six-and-thirty hours. "Waterbeach must be a wet place," I remarked to the honest ostler who was driving through the High-street of the village, meanwhile eyeing somewhat despondingly the thick, leaden-coloured clouds which were unstintingly emptying their watery treasures over the flat, far-spreading country. "Yes, sir," replied the man, at once catching my meaning, "it ain't called Waterbeach for nothing." On further enquiry it was readily found that the notion of the district never having been known to suffer to any considerable extent from drought was generally accepted. One authority was heard to venture the opinion that the weather never *would* clear up any more; while another gentleman, who had been a frequent visitor, declares that it always rains when he is there, go when he will. It may be all very well to ask, What's in a name? but cavil as we choose, Waterbeach is exceedingly suggestive, and our ancestors who framed the double word doubtless took into account the local characteristics of the country. Be this as it may, people naturally seem to associate the village with mists above and water below. It is not so very long since that a genius of a student, who was commissioned to "supply" the pulpit for a certain period, arrived on the ground provided with a complete oilskin outfit. Though the knowing might smile, "Waterbeach" was redolent of water; and he showed the wit of a growing theologian by being prepared for contingencies. Without presuming to speak as an authority, either one way or the other, I may add to the testimony of others that, having visited Waterbeach twice within the space of two years, it rained more or less on each occasion.

The object I had in view in visiting Waterbeach a second time was to see a veteran Baptist elder, named Robert Coe, who was a deacon of the church more than thirty years ago, when Mr. Spurgeon was pastor, and who then retained his honourable office. If Mr. Coe was not the *beau ideal* of a Nonconformist deacon, one's judgment must be awry; for he was hardly less than this to an unprejudiced Londoner interested in the "lions" and folk-lore of Old Cambridgeshire. The elder and his wife were found to be thorough country people, of the old-fashioned type; and while they were pious, thrifty, and well-to-do, they were so far animated by the predilections of a former generation that they were tempted to look askance on some of our valued modern contrivances. During the whole of their quiet, peaceful life they had not travelled any great distance from the family home; and, truth to say, they had never become completely satisfied with railway locomotion. Waterbeach was their world; and limited as the sphere might seem to natures of a more ambitious turn, Waterbeach had, under Providence, very sufficiently supplied their simple wants. If any are disposed to doubt the happiness of such a lot, their scepticism would vanish after they had spent an hour at the veteran's fireside. Mr. Coe was a successful man because he had done well as regards both worlds; and the restlessness of his eye was not the restlessness of discontent; it was rather the habit of a keen observer who could see through a visitor at a glance. He not only knew all about what had happened at Waterbeach during one or two generations, but he was quite willing to be communicative.

"Oh, what a sight of times he did try to get me to London," he remarked, passing his hand across his forehead and looking straight into the fire. "You mean Mr. Spurgeon?" "Yes," was the reply; "and he said, 'If you will come I will present you with a new flagon, and it shall be engraved.'" It transpired that a common black wine-bottle had been used at the communion table of the chapel opposite; and as such a practice could hardly be said to be either "decent" or "in order," the presentation of something better was suggested. The flagon was earned in due time, and I was privileged to hold the treasure in my hand, and to read the inscription, "Presented to the Baptist Church, Waterbeach, by C. H. Spurgeon, 1876."

The first visit of an elderly man to the metropolis, after he has spent his life in the country, is
a momentous event ; it is a very agitating piece
of experience.   The strangeness of everything
very naturally engenders a timidity such as he
has never felt before.   His uneasiness begins
when he finds himself seated in the " London
Express," and when the train attains its highest
speed he feels a disposition to stand and hold on
by the windows.   The excitement increases before
he has " done " a tithe part of the round of wonders
he is expected to see ; so that if at luncheon or
dinner he is caught in the act of using sugar with
potatoes, and salt with apple tart, the error is to
be attributed to the exceptional nature of the
surroundings.   When Mr. Coe actually visited
London he well survived a succession of shocks,
until a life longing was realised as he stood, on
a Sabbath morning, a unit in the great congregation at the Metropolitan Tabernacle.   " Robert, is
that you ? " said the Pastor at the close of the
service, without attempting to disguise his surprise
and delight ; " I thought I should never have
succeeded, but you are here at last ! "   The visitor
was entertained at Clapham ; he returned home
delighted with London, and more content than
ever with the quiet prosperity of Waterbeach.
Mr. Coe will never misinterpret these revelations

of his private life. He perhaps remembered that his position in the world was an exceptional one ; for, as one of Mr. Spurgeon's first deacons, thousands of people in both hemispheres were interested in his antecedents.

It appears that Mr. Spurgeon first went to Waterbeach in the fall of 1851, and ministered to the church during two years without having any fixed residence in the village. He succeeded Mr. Peters, who preached to the people for twenty-two years, the stipend through that period having been £5 a quarter. This venerable man was still living at Cambridge when I visited the neighbourhood ; and on one occasion, at the chapel anniversary, he grew warmly enthusiastic while speaking about old times. On such occasions there appears to be only one drawback to act as a damper on the natives' satisfaction—the old meeting-house is no more. One day, during the hot, dry weather of 1861, some careless person threw a quantity of hot ashes on a heap of litter hard by, and the result was that not only the chapel, but one or two other buildings, including an old workhouse, were totally consumed. "If it had not been burned the place would never have been pulled down," said Mr. Toller, who supplied the information, "for there were people there who venerated the very smoke." Mr. Spurgeon himself laid the

first stone of the present sanctuary, a few months
after the catastrophe.

Although it was then twenty-seven years ago,
my friend, Mr. Coe, still vividly remembered the
occasion of Mr. Spurgeon's first visit to Waterbeach on an autumn Sunday in 1851, the young
preacher having been commissioned to supply the
pulpit by an association at Cambridge, which
attended to the wants of neighbouring churches.
" He sat on one side of the table-pew, and I on
the other side," remarks the deacon, his face
beaming with pleasure as he recalls the scene.
" I shall never forget it.   He looked so white, and
I thought to myself *he'll* never be able to preach
—what a boy he is !   I despised his youth, you
know, and thought all this while the congregation
was singing.   Then, when the hymn was over, he
jumped up and began to read and expound the
chapter about the scribes and pharisees and
lawyers, and as he went on about their garments,
their phylacteries, and long prayers—I knew that
he *could* preach.   All along I was fully persuaded
in my own mind that he would not remain long
at Waterbeach.   I could see that he was something very great, and was evidently intended for
a larger sphere.   I could not make him out ; and
one day I asked him wherever he got all the
knowledge from that he put into the sermons.

' Oh,' he said, 'I take a book, and I pull the good things out of it by the hair of their heads.'"

Before its revival under Mr. Spurgeon's ministry the congregation at Waterbeach was very small, the chapel on ordinary occasions not being more than half filled ; but a new era of prosperity at once commenced. The empty seats were immediately taken, the aisles were invaded, the doors were surrounded by rustic crowds for whom there was no accommodation. One of Mr. Spurgeon's first deacons, a worthy of whom little is now to be learned, was named King, and for a time Mr. King was the Pastor's right-hand man. He has long since gone home to heaven. In those days the village bore an evil name on account of the drunkenness and profligacy which abounded ; now the inebriate appeared to be sobered, while transgressors of other sorts were awed into propriety. Because they could see that he was earnest and faithful, and had a kind heart, the most degraded of characters liked the new preacher, in spite of his terrible straight-forwardness in denouncing all kinds of evil. Mr. Coe remembered the sermons of those days ; and one especially—" How wilt thou do in the swelling of Jordan ? "—with its terrific warnings and solemn appeals, could never be effaced from memory. According to our informant it was truly wonderful how, thus early, Mr. Spurgeon thundered judgment against the sinner. After he had mellowed a little he seemed to grow milder; but, taking him for all in all, the like had never been heard in Cambridgeshire before. Though a thorough Calvinist, whose doctrines some thought at times to be rather high, his views at the outset were substantially the same as those preached to-day at the Tabernacle. He was from the first as faithful to ministers as to ordinary people, telling those who preached nothing save Election, without ever warning the sinner, that he should not like to stand in their shoes.

In the meantime, Deacon Coe was passing through one of the most enjoyable experiences of his life ; and his pleasure was only lessened by the consciousness that the sunshine could not last. If friends mentioned the matter to him, Deacon Coe would shake his · head in his characteristic expressive manner, and remark, " He will not be here long. God has a great work for him to do somewhere. I don't know where, but he will not be here long." Probably this opinion was shared by others in the little community ; at all events, the people seem to have made much of their youthful pastor, and to have hotly competed among themselves for the honour of according him a genuine hospitality. So numerous were the invitations to dinner that he never, during his tenure of office, went twice to the same place, the poor as well as the rich being allowed to take their turn. Thus, at a certain village lived a quaint worthy who was not despised on account of his poverty, and an invitation to take refreshment was accepted. At dinner a large pudding was placed on the table, and after the host had taken about a quarter of the same on his own plate he pushed the dish across the table with, " Now, friend, help yourself."

One or two of the Pastor's adventures during these early interesting years may be narrated. Much pleasure has been experienced in recovering them, and they will serve as material for a future biography.

At a certain date in the year 1852 Mr. Spurgeon was appointed to preach the anniversary sermons at a village chapel in the vicinity of Waterbeach, where the pastor was an octogenarian, a fine specimen of the old-fashioned school of dry, respectable, and orthodox ministers. The old gentleman adopted this course because he had heard of his young brother's popularity, although he had not seen his face, and he desired to attract a full congregation. When the preacher of the day arrived on the ground his extremely youthful

appearance created anything but a favourable
impression on the white-headed pastor who had
proclaimed the gospel in the neighbourhood
during forty years. " How do you do, Mr. ——— ?
I've come to preach your anniversary sermons,"
said the new comer, expecting the usual welcome.
" Ugh ! " replied the other, looking up somewhat
disconcerted, " I'm none the better for seeing *you.*"
Thinking that he was in a dilemma, and that the
anniversary would be a failure, the old pastor rose,
and, pacing the room, gave expression to his
impatience. " Tut, tut ! a pretty kettle of fish ;
boys going up and down the country preaching
before their mother's milk is well out of their
mouths." To the visitor all this naturally sounded
like somewhat strong language, and he inwardly
resolved that the veteran should hear of the
matter in another place. In the meantime the
crisis appeared to be all the more serious on
account of the numbers of people who were flocking into the village from all directions. As the
venerable pastor remarked, they were coming in
carts, they were coming in chaises, and they were
coming in buggies ; there would be an overflowing congregation. From Mr. Spurgeon's
standpoint there was nothing that could be done
other than for him to do his best, and to look for
the blessing of God : but this was so far from

being satisfactory to the pastor that he went about
the village still expressing his disgust at the idea
of boys being sent abroad to preach.   The
chapel was crowded at the time of service ; but
instead of yielding pleasure this fact seemed to
make the occasion still more unlucky.   At first
the old pastor retired into the background, where
he could not be seen.   A hymn was sung, and
the prayer was not quite what the judicious would
have expected from a mere boy.   Mr. Spurgeon
read Proverbs xvi., and when he came to "A
hoary head is a crown of glory," he showed that,
Solomon or no Solomon, it was not always so.
There were tongues in some hoary heads which
could not be civil to the boy who came to preach.
Rudeness gave no glory.   Then reading further—
if it be found in the way of righteousness—he
showed that Solomon was right after all, for
unless this were the case a man might as well
have red hair as white for a crown.   When the
sermon was over, the aged pastor, who had long
since come forth from his hiding-place, walked up
the pulpit stairs, opened the door, and as the boy-
preacher descended he received a smart, playful
slap on the loins, accompanied with the com-
plimentary remark, "You are the sauciest dog
that ever barked in a pulpit."   Instead of com-
plaining of his " supply," Mr. —— now went, first

4

to one and then another, expressing his wonder and delight, seeing such an extraordinary youth had appeared in their midst.

The above is an example of the mistakes that may be made by those who too readily despise a preacher's youth ; and, according to Deacon Coe, Mr. Spurgeon's trials in this respect were exceptionally heavy ; but neither in youth nor later on in life did he ever retaliate.

There were "characters" to be found at Waterbeach in those days, and among them was a man who, although he was worth some thousands of pounds, was at last buried in his own garden "to save expense." On a certain Sabbath morning this individual placed seven shillings and sixpence in the Pastor's hand with some such remark as, " Please accept this ; you want a hat." On the following Sunday he brought an additional half-crown. " What is this for ? " asked Mr. Spurgeon, surprised at receiving a supplemental offering. Then came a singular confession —" Last week the Lord told me to give you ten shillings ; but I kept back half-a-crown, and there it is." The tradition in Waterbeach is, that a hat was purchased with this money.

On a certain summer evening Mr. Spurgeon had engaged to preach at Teversham, which lies a short distance from Waterbeach ; but before he could reach his destination the sky darkened, and a severe thunder-storm burst over the country. While passing a cottage on the road a woman was observed to be alarmed and in sore distress on account of the tempest ; and not liking to pass on and leave a fellow-creature in trouble, Mr. Spurgeon entered the house, read a few verses, then prayed, and so comforted the woman while the storm continued. Having done this piece of service, he proceeded to Teversham to fulfil the engagement ; but found that the chapel was closed and dark, for people were not expecting a sermon on account of the tempest. Mr. Spurgeon wore a waterproof coat, and on entering the village he divested himself of this, because the smooth surface seemed to reflect the vivid flashes of lightning in a way that might alarm the timid. He then went round from door to door, and told the people there would be a service, and advised them to assemble in the meeting-house. The summons was obeyed with alacrity, the sermon was preached, and when all was over the young pastor started on his homeward walk to Cambridge, a distance of four miles.

"A Wesleyan Minister," writing about twenty years ago, in speaking of Mr. Spurgeon's early days, remarks : " He removed from Newmarket to Cambridge in the capacity of usher to his old

friend and former tutor, Henry Leeding.   Here
both his earthly comforts and religious privileges
were increased.   He now began publicly to
exhort, and united himself with a society called
the Lay Preachers' Association, connected with
the church in St. Andrew's Street, formerly under
the pastorate of the illustrious Robert Hall.   At
a little village called Teversham, in a cottage
some miles from Cambridge, he preached his
first sermon, when only sixteen years of age.
His preaching from the beginning was highly
acceptable, and his sermons were illustrated by
geography and astronomy . . . and, to his praise
be it recorded, the common people heard him
gladly.   But he was pre-eminently liked by the
members of a small church at a village called
Waterbeach, who, perceiving this germ of uncommon talents, invited him to become their
pastor.   And here, in a rude chapel made out
of a barn, with a high pitched roof, he preached
every Sabbath in the forenoon and afternoon.
When requested to preach also in the evening,
he modestly replied, "I cannot always preach
three times, for I am not so strong as a man."

It would have been a satisfaction to many who
are now interested in taking a retrospect if the
sermons of Mr. Spurgeon's earliest days had been
preserved.   There was a time when he himself

thought of presenting the public with a selection, for in 1857 he wrote: "I shall soon issue a volume of my earliest productions while pastor at Waterbeach, and would now bespeak for it a favourable reception." We are not aware that this publication ever appeared.

Such are a few of the things associated with Waterbeach which I was enabled to recover through the kindness of friends on the spot and from others. The church was found to be in a flourishing condition, and the stipend of the pastor was probably double what it was in Mr. Spurgeon's time.

To these, however, may be added the following, relating to these times, and told by Mr. Spurgeon himself in *The Spare Half Hour :*—

" Having to preach at one of the village stations of the Cambridge Lay Preachers' Association, I walked slowly in a meditative frame of mind over Midsummer Common to the little wooden bridge which leads to Chesterton, and in the midst of the common I was startled by what seemed a loud voice, but which may have been a singular illusion ; whichever it was, the impression was vivid to an intense degree : I seemed very distinctly to hear the words, 'Seekest thou great things for thyself ? Seek them not !' This led me to look at my position from another point of view, and to challenge my motives and intentions. I remembered the poor but loving people to whom I ministered, and the souls which had been given me in my humble charge, and although at that time I anticipated obscurity and poverty as the result of the resolve, yet I did there and then solemnly renounce the offer of collegiate instruction, determining to abide for a season at least with my people, and to remain preaching the Word so long as I had strength to do it. Had it not been for those words, in all probability I had never been where and what I now am. I was conscientious in my obedience to the monition, and I have never seen cause to regret it.

"Waiting upon the Lord for direction will never fail to afford us timely intimations of His will ; for though the ephod is no more worn by a ministering priest, the Lord still guides His people by His wisdom, and orders all their paths in love ; and in times of perplexity, He makes them to hear a voice behind them, saying, 'This is the way, walk ye in it.'"

THE FIRST SUNDAYS IN LONDON.

"*Before any great achievement*, some measure of . . . depression is very usual. Surveying the difficulties before us, our hearts sink within us. The sons of Anak stalk before us, and we are as grass-hoppers in our own sight in their presence. The cities of Canaan are walled up to heaven, and who are we that we should hope to capture them? We are ready to cast down our weapons and take to our heels. Nineveh is a great city, and we would flee unto Tarshish sooner than encounter its noisy crowds. Already we look for a ship which may bear us quietly away from the terrible scene, and only a dread of tempest restrains our recreant footsteps. Such was my experience when I first became a pastor in London. My success appalled me; and the thought of the career which it seemed to open up, so far from elating me, cast me into the lowest depth, out of which I uttered my *miserere* and found no room for a *gloria in excelsis*. Who was I that I should continue to lead so great a multitude? I would betake me to my village obscurity, or emigrate to America, and find a solitary rest in the back woods where I might be sufficient for the things which would be demanded of me. . . . I felt myself a mere child, and trembled as I heard the voice which said, 'Arise, and thresh the mountains, and make them as chaff.'"—*Lectures to my Students*, i. 173.

III.

THE FIRST SUNDAYS IN LONDON.

WHAT people call accident is frequently the course of events as pre-ordained by God ; and the truth of this remark was strikingly proved in the manner of Mr. Spurgeon's general rearing. The more carefully we look into the surrounding circumstances of his early life, the more clearly shall we see that all things were working together for good to equip the child and the youth for his arduous life-work that lay beyond. His parents, and the generation preceding them, were not only Christians of an old-fashioned type, they were professors who made no secret of their Puritanic sympathies. Even the prophet Samuel could hardly have enjoyed more tender nurture and careful training to fit him for future service in the Lord's house. The father was a preacher, so also was the grandfather ; and one of Mr. Spurgeon's earliest recollections belongs to his sitting on a hassock in the study of the latter, looking at the missionary pictures in *The Evan-*

gelical Magazine, not ever presuming to make a
noise, lest grandfather should be interrupted in
making his sermon, and thus be unable to preach,
when no good would be done, and Charles would
be the offender. On account of the uncompromising old-fashioned notions entertained by the
family in religious matters, the opinion that the
Pastor commenced work as a lame scholar may
have gained currency. The truth is, that at a
very early age his scholarship was not only far
above the average, but very conspicuous to all
who had eyes to discern. This happens to be
a subject on which we can speak with authority ;
for some time ago Mr. Spurgeon made some
passing remarks relating to his former tutor, which
were quite new and conclusive. During some
years past the gentleman in question had resided
in a southern suburb, unknown to his former
scholar ; and, like some others of his profession,
found the new Board-schools serious drawbacks
to his day-school. He is, however, a thoroughly
able teacher, who would be invaluable to anyone
who should seek out and obtain the benefit of
his instructions. This gentleman, who may be
regarded as a thoroughly competent judge, held
very clear and decided views in regard to the
attainments of his quondam pupil. He was in a
position to set those right who went about retail-

ing the news that Spurgeon was no scholar ; for in point of fact, the said Spurgeon, as a mere youth, was one of the most competent scholars in the neighbourhood of Cambridge, and one who could easily have taken a degree at the University without undergoing the process of cramming. While he spoke like a man who was reasonably proud of his former charge, the venerable tutor was not of the genus which can tolerate cross-examination or interviewings.

Perhaps it never occurred to those who spread the report about Mr. Spurgeon being no scholar, that at the time of his first coming to London he was very competently earning a livelihood by his scholarship. In addition to the Waterbeach church he received a salary as usher in a school at Cambridge, and afterwards salary as tutor to a couple of youths in the same neighbourhood. Very few indeed of our Nonconformist students at seventeen could show the same amount of knowledge ; and his habits of reading, in pulling the best things out of books " by the hair of their heads," enabled him to rapidly increase his stores.

It should also be generally known that Mr. Spurgeon was popular even as a boy ; for when in his turn he would address the Sunday-school at Newmarket, many members of the church

would secrete themselves in any convenient hole
or corner within earshot, and there eagerly listen
to his earliest efforts. On the other hand, there
were those among the Nonconformists of the
town who, through being unable to see excellence
in any form, supposed that the young preacher
was not only not a genius, but decidedly below
the average in every respect. When he first
came to New Park Street Chapel there arose
a great chatter among the Baptists of a certain
important town. Said one leading elder to a
brother officer of a similar calibre to himself,
" They have invited Charley Spurgeon to London,
and they are actually going to pay him £150
a-year!" A more curious misjudgment never
came out of Essex; and to add to its impressive-
ness, the words were drawn out to unnatural
length, as though the speaker's vocabulary were
as elastic as his notions were modest.

A good deal has been said at different times
about Mr. Spurgeon's conversion; and some in-
genious endeavours have been made to trace the
preacher of the sermon which was the means of
bringing peace to his soul. All that is really
known, however, about the preacher is, that he
was a Primitive Methodist in Colchester, and a
working man. The things spoken about were
the end of all things; the most unlikely people

to be saved ; the most despairing ; the most sinful ; and then it was shown that salvation is not by works, but by faith—the soul must look at Christ, and do so in a way corresponding to the perception of natural objects by the natural eye. After hearing this sermon he experienced the peace of God which passes all understanding, and went forth in strength to begin his life-work.

How Mr. Spurgeon first came to London is a question that has not always been correctly answered, and the causes which worked together to bring about the Pastor's removal to an enlarged sphere of labour are known only to a few persons. Let me narrate the circumstances as concisely as possible.

There can be no doubt that Waterbeach was a very comfortable sphere of labour for a young man like Mr. Spurgeon. Though the people were homely they had warm hearts, and they cordially appreciated their pastor's energy and eloquence. It is not impossible that some among the good farmers and simple peasants who crowded the chapel may have reckoned on a life-long union. At any rate, it is unreasonable to suppose that everybody detected in their accomplished pastor the surprising talents that he really possessed. Others were more far-sighted ; they were happy ; their church flourished ; but, alas ! it was con-

trary to the ordinary run of things for the great
outside world—a selfish world, as it must have
appeared to the Baptists of Waterbeach—to
allow so unequal a union to exist for lack of
a suitable opening being found elsewhere.

The fact was, that an ancient church, and
formerly a congregation of some importance in
the capital, was in great straits for want of a
pastor. Two centuries before, that church had
been formed by a band of Puritan Baptists, the
first pastor of whom we have any account being
William Rider. The divines who afterwards
successively held the pastorate, during a great
number of years, were all men of power and
celebrity : Benjamin Keach is still kept in remembrance by his *Metaphors ;* Benjamin Stinton
was equally worthy ; John Gill was a celebrated
commentator ; John Rippon was the compiler of
the hymn-book named after him ; Joseph Angus
is a successful tutor and author of our own times ;
James Smith was an uneducated genius of fervent
piety. In the chequered history of this old
church it has been a favourable omen for the
pastor to be chosen at the age of nineteen. It
was so with John Gill, and also with his successor, John Rippon, who were the only pastors
during the unusually long period of one hundred
and seventeen years. Mr. Spurgeon was of this

same auspicious age of nineteen when some one carried word to the despairing deacons at New Park Street Chapel that there was a young man making some stir at Waterbeach, and it was just possible he might resuscitate their cause.

The church at this date was slowly dying a natural death, and it was worth while to grasp at a straw if, thereby, the threatened death could be averted. It so happened that Mr. Olney, one of the deacons at New Park Street thirty-three years ago, was acquainted with a gentleman of the name of Gould, and on a certain occasion Mr. Gould's nephew happened to look in at a Baptist Chapel in Cambridge, at which a meeting was being held. On the platform were a couple of elderly ministers and a full-faced youth of more tender years. In due course the younger man made a speech, and, because he spoke as a Calvinist, what he said had the effect of highly displeasing those who considered that they were his elders and his betters. They had not even the good sense to keep their anger to themselves, but each had his say. One thought that Mr. Spurgeon should tarry at Jericho till his beard was grown ; the other wished to know why the young Baptist had left his few sheep in the wilderness ; he had surely come up to see the battle. A reply was made, and one which was very characteristic of the speaker at that time, but unfortunately this has not been recovered.

In course of time the news spread that a young Baptist minister had been snubbed down in Cambridgeshire ; and, as the declining church at New Park Street was then in want of a pastor, here was an· opportunity to secure a promising man. " I wish you would send for him, I believe he would suit you," remarked the informant, and the deacon at once felt disposed to make the experiment recommended.   Mr. Olney wrote at once to Mr. Spurgeon, who, however, manifested no particular anxiety to visit the great metropolis. When he first received the letter he thought a mistake had been made, and thus sent on the epistle to another pastor of the same name ; but it was at once returned with the intimation—" It is not a mistake : you are the man intended." Still he was in no hurry to settle in London. Only a short time before, while walking near Chesterton, he had been startled by what seemed like a voice speaking, " Seekest thou great things for thyself ? seek them not ;" and this remarkable circumstance, which fixed the young preacher's determination not to enter Stepney College, may have checked the rising of any ambitious aspirations connected with a London settlement.   At all events, he did not consent to preach at New

Park Street Chapel until an application for him to do so had been repeatedly made ; and when at length he came forth from the seclusion of Cambridgeshire, he came in no very sanguine mood. Nor was this a matter for surprise. The Church at New Park Street was not so flourishing as it had been ; and in the estimation of out-siders, who were disposed to take a desponding view of the situation, nothing very far short of a miracle could save the cause from ultimate decay. There were deacons of piety and substance, and a congregation of a hundred or more ; but, not-withstanding, what man of common prudence, or of common sense—especially at nineteen years of age—would be likely to hazard leading the for-lorn hope of filling twelve hundred empty seats, or of imparting life to a cause which was richer in illustrious memories than in present resources ? But Mr. Spurgeon was invited, and, to the great delight of the church, he accepted the invitation. When he entered the vestry he asked which was Dr. Gill's chair, and on seating himself in that interesting relic he exclaimed, "He must needs go through Samaria." This showed the Calvin-istic tendencies of his mind, and also the de-sponding view he took of a London settlement. "I knew that I should be of no use to you," he added, " but you would have me come."

On the Sabbath morning of Mr. Spurgeon's
first preaching at New Park Street, only the
average congregation was present, and many,
when for the first time they cast their eyes on
his youthful features, were not cheered. " What
a boy !" was the thought uppermost in the minds
of not a few judicious souls. His first text was
James i. 17 : " Every good gift and every perfect
gift is from above," etc. Was it to be expected
that a boy could turn that valley of dry bones
into a garden of the Lord ?

In the evening the congregation had very
perceptibly increased, but even then it was only
by degrees that the staid members gained confidence. When he turned to Revelation vii. and
began to read, and then to expound, thoughts
of misgiving arose in the hearts of some. What
an absurd thing, mused one experienced Christian who was present, for such a boy to turn to
such a passage as that of the hundred and forty
and four thousand, who were sealed unto ever-
lasting life. He became reassured, however, as
the preacher proceeded with his comments.
Then came the text and the sermon : " They
are without fault before the throne of God."
It would be impossible to describe the emotions
of the congregation as the discourse proceeded,
and the preacher warmed with his subject. One

who was present assures us that the effect was
amazing. Nearly all the members of the old
church were át last raised from their condition
of despondency ; although it is possible that
some were present who could not all at once
become reconciled to the preacher's bold departure from pulpit conventionalities. From the
first the commenting struck people as being even
more extraordinary than the sermons.

After the service was ended, the congregation
were too excited to leave the chapel and go
home. In all parts of the building they were
seen in groups conversing about what they had
heard, and of Mr. Spurgeon's eligibility for the
pastorate. The deacons had to come forth from
the vestry and promise that they would use their
endeavours to secure the young preacher. I have
also been informed that a church meeting was
arranged for to be held as soon as possible,
when an invitation to Mr. Spurgeon to accept
the pastorate was adopted. The invitation was
unanimous with the exception of one dissentient,
an elderly deacon, who quietly left immediately
after the pastor's settlement.

One other reminiscence of that memorable day
must be recorded. Mr. Thomas Olney, the senior
deacon, and his wife Unity—whose name is kept
in remembrance by one of the Orphanage houses

at Stockwell—at that time resided at Croydon ; and, partly because she was an invalid, it was not Mrs. Olney's practice to attend New Park Street Chapel when no one save a "nobody" was to preach.   On the occasion of Mr. Spurgeon's first coming Mrs. Olney did not undertake the journey from Croydon to Southwark, on account of what she judged to be very valid reasons. Who was the preacher for the day?   Oh, nobody but a young man from Waterbeach, in Cambridgeshire—a little village, and the last place under the sun likely to have an attractive preacher for its pastor.   When Mr. Olney returned home in the middle of the day his face beamed with pleasure, and the sparkle of his eye told that his heart was filled with gladness. At last when he spoke he said to his wife, "We have such a wonderful young man come to preach to-day ; you must come to chapel to-night." The old lady went to New Park Street as desired, and the good impression produced on her mind was as deep as it was lasting.   "He will do," she said, on her return to Croydon, and, with her own peculiar emphasis, "*He* will do."   Was not Mrs. Olney right?

In addition to the above we must not overlook the reminiscences which Mr. Spurgeon has himself given in *The Sword and the Trowel* for

January 1879. The article is entitled "Twenty-
five Years Ago," and the following are its
opening paragraphs, which directly refer to the
first visit to London in the last days of 1853 :—

" *Twenty-five years ago* we walked on a Sabbath
morning, according to our wont, from Cambridge
to the village of Waterbeach, in order to occupy
the pulpit of the little Baptist Chapel. It was a
country road, and there were four or five honest
miles of it, which we usually measured each
Sunday foot by foot, unless we happened to be
met by a certain little pony and cart which came
half way, but could not by any possibility venture
further, because of the enormous expense which
would have been incurred by driving through the
toll-gate at Milton. That winter's morning we
were all aglow with our walk, and ready for our
pulpit exercises. Sitting down in the table-pew,
a letter was passed to us bearing the postmark
of London. It was an unusual missive, and was
opened with curiosity. It contained an invitation to preach at New Park Street Chapel,
Southwark, the pulpit of which had formerly been
occupied by Dr. Rippon,—the very Dr. Rippon
whose hymn-book was then before us upon the
table—the great Dr. Rippon, out of whose Selection we were about to choose hymns for our
worship. The late Dr. Rippon seemed to hover

over us as an immeasurably great man, the glory of whose name covered New Park Street Chapel and its pulpit with awe unspeakable. We quietly passed the letter across the table to the deacon who gave out the hymns, observing that there was some mistake, and that the letter must have been intended for a Mr. Spurgeon who preached somewhere down in Norfolk. He shook his head, and observed that he was afraid there was no mistake, as he always knew that his minister would be run away with by some large church or other, but that he was a little surprised that the Londoners should have heard of him quite so soon. 'Had it been Cottenham, or St. Ives, or Huntingdon,' said he, 'I should not have wondered at all ; but going to London is rather a great step from this little place.' He shook his head very gravely ; but the time was come for us to look out the hymns, and therefore the letter was put away, and, as far as we can remember, was for the day quite forgotten, even as a dead man out of mind.

" On the following Monday an answer was sent to London, informing the deacon of the church at Park Street that he had fallen into an error in directing his letter to Waterbeach, for the Baptist minister of that village was very little more than nineteen years of age, and quite unqualified to occupy a London pulpit. In due time came another epistle, setting forth that the former letter had been written in perfect knowledge of the young preacher's age, and had been intended for him, and him alone. The request of the former letter was repeated and pressed, a date mentioned for the journey to London, and the place appointed at which the preacher would find lodging. That invitation was accepted, and as the result thereof the boy preacher of the Fens took his post in London.

" *Twenty-five years ago*—and yet it seems but yesterday—we lodged for the night at a boarding-house in Queen Square, Bloomsbury, to which the worthy deacon directed us. As we wore a huge black satin stock, and used a blue handkerchief with white spots, the young gentlemen of that boarding-house marvelled · greatly at the youth from the country who had come up to preach in London, but who was evidently in the condition known as verdant green. They were mainly of the evangelical church persuasion, and seemed greatly tickled that the country lad should be a preacher. They did not propose to go and hear the youth, but they seemed to tacitly agree to *encourage* him after their own fashion, and we were encouraged accordingly. What tales were narrated of the great divines of the metropolis,

and their congregations !   One we remember had
a thousand *city* men to hear him, another had his
church filled with *thoughtful* people, such as could
hardly be matched all over England, while a third
had an immense audience, almost entirely composed of the *young men* of London, who were
spell-bound by his eloquence.   The study which
these men underwent in composing their sermons,
their herculean toils in keeping up their congregations, and the matchless oratory which they
exhibited on all occasions, were duly rehearsed in
our hearing, and when we were shown to bed in
a cupboard over the front door, we were not in
an advantageous condition for pleasant dreams.
Park Street hospitality never sent the young
minister to that far-away hired room again, but
assuredly the Saturday evening in a London
boarding-house was about the most depressing
agency which could have been brought to bear
upon our spirit.   On the narrow bed we tossed
in solitary misery, and found no pity.   Pitiless
was the grind of the cabs in the street, pitiless
the recollection of the young city clerks whose
grim propriety had gazed upon our rusticity with
such amusement, pitiless the spare room which
scarce afforded space to kneel, pitiless even the
gas-lamps which seemed to wink at us as they
flickered amid the December darkness.   We had

no friend in all that city full of human beings, but we felt among strangers and foreigners, hoped to be helped through the scrape into which we had been brought, and to escape safely to the serene abodes of Cambridge and Waterbeach, which then seemed to be Eden itself.

" *Twenty-five years ago* it was a clear, cold morning, and we wended our way along Holborn Hill towards Blackfriars and certain tortuous lanes and alleys at the foot of Southwark Bridge. Wondering, praying, fearing, hoping, believing,— we felt all alone and yet not alone. Expectant of Divine help, and inwardly borne down by our sense of the need of it, we traversed a dreary wilderness of brick to find the spot where our message must needs be delivered. One word rose to our lip many times, we scarce know why —' He must needs go through Samaria.' The necessity of our Lord's journeying in a certain direction is no doubt repeated in His servants, and as our present journey was not of our seeking, and had been by no means pleasing so far as it had gone—the one thought of a " needs be " for it seemed to overtop every other. At sight of Park Street Chapel we felt for a moment amazed at our own temerity, for it seemed to our eyes to be a large, ornate, and imposing structure, suggesting an audience wealthy and critical, and far removed from the humble folk to whom our ministry had been sweetness and light.   It was early, so there were no persons entering, and when the set time was fully come there were no signs to support the suggestion raised by the exterior of the building, and we felt that by God's help we were not yet out of our depth, and were not likely to be with so small an audience.   The Lord helped us very graciously, we had a happy Sabbath in the pulpit, and spent the intervals with warm-hearted friends ; and when at night we trudged back to the Queen Square narrow lodging we were not alone, and we no longer looked on Londoners as flinty-hearted barbarians. Our tone was altered, we wanted no pity of anyone, we did not care a penny for the young gentlemen lodgers and their miraculous ministers, nor for the grind of the cabs, nor for anything else under the sun.   The lion had been looked at all round, and his majesty did not appear to be a tenth as majestic as when we had only heard his roar miles away."

So far as I have been sufficiently fortunate to recover them, the incidents related are those which were associated with Mr. Spurgeon's first Sabbath-day's work in London in the fall of the year 1853.   The congregations immediately increased until the chapel was densely thronged at every service ; and the building was then enlarged to accommodate some eighteen hundred people. The more they knew of their Pastor the more did the church and congregation learn to appreciate his public service and personal worth ; but it was otherwise with outsiders of the same denomination, who were either too undiscerning or too jealous to see and acknowledge the truth.

There were many who were still partial to old-fashioned ways, and these had misgivings. Could they only get another Rippon all might yet be well—the tide of prosperity would return ; but what could be made of the bold Essex youth of nineteen, whose daring originality was shocking to people who had beheld the propriety reflected in the portraits of Gill and Rippon ?

It is an interesting question, What did the preacher appear like at this time ? The query is thus answered by an American quarterly for the year 1859: " He was unpractised in either the art of oratory or of preaching, his public efforts having consisted of addresses before Sunday-schools, and a very brief but successful pastorate over an obscure Baptist church at Waterbeach. In personal appearance he was not prepossessing ; in style he was plain, practical, simple ; in manner, rude, bold, egotistical, approaching to the bigoted ; in theology, a deep-dyed Calvinist ; in church relations, an uncompromising Baptist. We could scarcely imagine a more unpromising list of qualifications, or rather disqualifications, for public favour."

Such was the man, as viewed by a discriminating judge at a distance ; what were his associations at home and his prospects in the metropolis ? The chapel in New Park Street seated twelve hundred persons, and for some time past a sixth part of that number made an average congregation. The revival was, of course, immediate. The good souls who were present at the first scantily-attended service, and who, according to their nervous temperament, professed to be shocked or edified, carried the news of the altered aspect of affairs to others, and thus helped to bring together ever-increasing crowds. Ever after this day of small things the aforesaid good souls were sorely inconvenienced by having less elbow-room, and a more limited supply of pure air, than they had been accustomed to enjoy in olden time. The chapel became suddenly crowded as no other London chapel had ever been known to be—that is to say, the throng, which weekly filled aisles and pews, manifested a determined sort of eagerness to see and hear the preacher. This was the aspect of affairs in

London when the deacons said, "Come amongst us for six months."

Waterbeach was, at least, a sufficient contrast to all this excitement and popularity for Mr. Spurgeon to call it, on his return, "this little Garden of Eden." He loved his people ; he experienced uncomfortable sensations in being called upon to leave them ; and, had not poverty denied him freedom of action, he would "have turned a deaf ear to any request to leave them." As, however, the little church was unable to afford him adequate support, he was impelled forward by necessity. The engagement at Waterbeach could be terminated at any time by either party after the expiration of a three-months' notice ; but pastor and people were bound together in closer union than could ever have been effected by legal forms. At the outset, he showed no symptoms of being carried away by that amazing popularity which immediately confronted him. In a letter to Mr. Lowe, he commended the people on account of their prudence in allotting an ample term of proba-tion, while at the same time he declined to bind himself for longer than three months. If all progressed well, the engagement could easily be prolonged ; if otherwise, he "would only be a 'supply'—liable to a fortnight's dismissal or resignation." The deacons at London said, "Come at once;" those at Waterbeach were quite averse to so sudden a termination of their connection, and in this respect carried their point. The regular pastorate of Mr. Spurgeon in London may be said to have begun on the 27th of April, 1854. He immediately achieved an unexampled popularity for one so young ; but neither pastor nor people could have had even a faint idea as to what lay before them in the future.

As this is not a complete history, it will not be necessary to give a connected account of subsequent events. These are told by Mr. Spurgeon himself in his book on the Tabernacle, and anything which is included in that volume is not likely to be news to readers of these pages. How the old chapel at New Park Street became crowded so as to warrant an adjournment to Exeter Hall, and subsequently to the Music Hall at the Royal Surrey Gardens, where an appalling accident saddened the church and prostrated the preacher, are things too well known to need recapitulation.

In "The Treasury of David," under Psalm xci., there is a less-known reminiscence of the eventful first year in London, which is too characteristic to be omitted. The country, it will be remembered, was stricken with the fever engendered by the Russian war, when the sickness referred to was raging :—

"In the year 1854, when I had scarcely been in London twelve months, the neighbourhood in which I laboured was visited by Asiatic cholera, and my congregation suffered from its inroads. Family after family summoned me to the bedsides of the smitten, and almost every day I was called to visit the grave. I gave myself up with youthful ardour to the visitation of the sick, and was sent for from all corners of the district by persons of all ranks and religions. I became weary in body and sick at heart. My friends seemed falling one by one, and I felt or fancied that I was sickening like those around me. A little more work and weeping would have laid me low among the rest. I felt that my burden was heavier than I could bear, and I was ready to sink under it. As God would have it, I was returning mournfully home from a funeral, when my curiosity led me to read a paper which was wafered up in a shoemaker's window in the Dover Road. It did not look like a trade announcement, nor was it ; for it bore in a good bold handwriting these words :—' *Because thou hast made the Lord, which is my refuge, even the Most High, thy habitation, there shall no evil befall thee, neither shall any plague come nigh thy dwelling.*' The effect upon

my heart was immediate.   Faith appropriated the
passage as her own.   I felt secure, refreshed, girt
with immortality.   I went on with my visitation
of the dying in a calm and peaceful spirit; I felt
no fear of evil, and I suffered no harm.   The
Providence which moved the tradesman to place
those verses in his window I gratefully acknowledge, and in the remembrance of its marvellous
power I adore the Lord my God."

That a special Providence watched over the
youthful pastor during the trials of that first
terrible summer in London, no one will doubt
after reading of the above adventure.   Only a
man with a large admixture of heroism in his
nature could have faced the ordeal to come off in
the end a conqueror.

When Mr. Spurgeon first settled in London
in the spring of 1854, the news of his success
soon reached the ears of quiet-living folks in
every rural nook in England.   Well do I remember how his fame found its way into the
secluded Somersetshire village where I was then
residing, when of course the village politicians
each formed an independent opinion.   What a
talk there was about his work, and about the
daring originality of his manner of doing it!
The sermons were read with avidity; for neither
the young, who were ready to welcome something

new, nor the more elderly, who still venerated
William Jay and John Angell James as models
of pulpit propriety, had ever seen words put
together in such a way before. When Macaulay
first appeared in *The Edinburgh Review* the
question was, "Where did he get that style?"
and a similar query might have been started when
the new preacher suddenly burst upon the world
in 1854. In a certain instance a pastor went to
one of his brethren who served a church four
miles away, and, having mentioned the fact that
he had read one of Mr. Spurgeon's latest sermons,
he added, "but he can never keep on like this."
The reference was to the prodigality of thought
and to the number of illustrations diffused throughout the discourses ; and as the publication proceeded the old worthy thought he had discovered
a falling off, as he had predicted there would be.

Persons of strong sense and penetrative judgment were enabled at once to see Mr. Spurgeon's
worth, but weaker men required a longer time
for their opinions to become settled. What was
most surprising was the singular behaviour of one
or two leading Baptist ministers in London, whose
open hostility to the man who was manifestly
raised up for a great work had the effect of
making both themselves and their clique ridiculous.
As it was with individuals, so was it with the

6

newspapers. The weaklings hesitated—they were neither supporters nor detractors of Mr. Spurgeon; but stronger natures, such as the *The Morning Advertiser*, assumed a bold front, and gained considerable credit in the long run for the sagacity which enabled them to arrive at a common-sense decision.

Though he differed on many doctrinal points from Mr. Spurgeon, the late Dr. Binney was able from the first to perceive the great talents of the young preacher. On a particular occasion, as I have learned, when he was visiting one of the Independent colleges for the purpose of giving a lecture to the students, the Weighhouse pastor happened to hear some disparaging remarks concerning Mr. Spurgeon from certain of the students. The lecturer asked them to be quiet, to listen to what he himself had to say on the matter, and addressed them in such words as these : " I myself have enjoyed some amount of popularity; I have always been able to draw together a congregation ; but in the person of Mr. Spurgeon we see a young man, be he who he may, and come whence he will, who at twenty-four hours' notice can command a congregation of twenty thousand people. Now, I have never been able to do that, and I never knew of anyone else who could do it." Mr. Spurgeon could do greater things than Dr. Binney, or all the efforts of the students combined could do, and on that account there was wisdom in remaining quiet, and withholding railing words.

One of the earliest sermons preached by Mr. Spurgeon in London was from the text, " Fear not, thou worm Jacob." It was a discourse of great power, and was one which seemed at once to establish the preacher's fame. It was, moreover, one of the series which were to have been probationary sermons ; but, in reality, it can hardly be said that Mr. Spurgeon ever preached any probationary sermons at all. His very first Sabbath day's work in the metropolis settled the matter of his unanimous call to the pastorate.

I have heard it said by one of its oldest members that the church at New Park Street was as much prepared for the reception of Mr. Spurgeon by providence as Mr. Spurgeon was prepared for the position. The church was in a low condition, however ; and although there were two hundred members, no one knew where to find them. There was a good chapel, and there was a staff of well-to-do deacons to second the efforts of the pastor ; but had Mr. Spurgeon been an optimist the outlook would have been discouraging to the last degree.

When he suddenly became popular in London,

applications for Mr. Spurgeon's services began
to pour in from the provinces. His days were,
accordingly, days of travel and adventure, and his
own words, spoken in 1855, give a more vivid
picture of his experience at this time than any
other description. Referring to a northern tour
he said : " Many persons know that on my road
home I was exposed to very imminent danger.   I
crossed the river Clyde in a ferry : the man who
had the management of the boat had taken 'a
wee drap o' the cratur,' and was not able to
manage it at all, and had put twenty-six persons
into a boat that ought to have contained far less.
I have been informed by one or two ladies that
report was current that I was thrown into the
water, and fished up by the hair of my head.
Now, that was not so. We were simply in
danger, but by a little management and expostu-
lation, which was resented by oaths and curses,
we came safe to land.   Thanks to that God who
both on sea and land cares for His people ! I had
engaged to preach in Bradford, in Yorkshire.   I
first made a journey to Lake Windermere, round
which I sailed, and greatly enjoyed the beauties
of its scenery. I went to Bradford, and on
Sabbath morning I found they had engaged the
music-hall, which holds, they say, a thousand
persons more than Exeter Hall. Instead of

being able to contain the crowds who came on Sunday, about as many had to go away as were accommodated. In the evening the streets presented a solid blockade of men and women. The place was crammed to excess, and I had scarcely room to walk about to deliver what I had to say to the people. . . . I went to Stockton-on-Tees, and there again preached the word of God to a very numerous congregation. I journeyed on still further, to Edinburgh, and in Queen Street Hall, notwithstanding the most pouring rains, more crowds were assembled." Thus in one town after another great crowds were attracted, and on one occasion, in Glasgow, it was said that twenty thousand persons went away unable to obtain admission.

It was not long before the crowds in front of New Park Street Chapel filled the street. Then Exeter Hall and Surrey Gardens' Hall were successively taken, but more because they afforded a larger sphere of usefulness than from any other reason. The profits from the services of the last-named place aided in some considerable degree the Tabernacle building fund. It is not generally known that the Tabernacle very narrowly escaped being erected on leasehold land ; and that what would have been a real disaster was prevented by certain of the deacons refusing to sign the building contract on such conditions. The site was in possession of the Fishmongers' Company; and Mr. Joynson, of St. Mary Cray, became a main instrument under providence in obtaining the freehold. Thus, as we hope, THE METROPOLITAN TABERNACLE can remain until the end of time as a monument of the sanctified' genius and earnest life-work of C. H. SPURGEON.

PERSONAL REMINISCENCES.

"Our life has been mainly spent in *direct* religious teaching, and to that work we would dedicate our main strength ; but men need also to hear common every-day things spoken of in a religious manner, for to some of them this roundabout road is the only way to their hearts. Theology is dull reading to the unconverted ; but mixed with a story, or set forth by a witty saying, they will drink in a great amount of religious truth and find no fault. They like their pills gilded, or at least sugar-coated, and if by that means they may be really benefited, who will grudge them the gilt or the sugar?"—*Preface to The Spare Half-Hour.*

IV.

WHAT others say about a man must be estimated according to the personal worth and sympathies of the speakers ; but what a man says about himself is sure, one way or the other, to be a revelation of character. While no one will defend egotism, it is possible for conceit or spurious humility to conceal itself in a reticence, foolish because studied and unnatural. He must be a shrewd judge both of himself and others who can constantly make capital of himself, while it is still evident that self is not mentioned for the sake of glorification. It must be evident to every observer that from the first Mr. Spurgeon has been to himself an exhaustless book of illustration, many of the most telling things in his sermons and lectures being personal reminiscences. Anecdotes of childhood and of later age are continually appearing, without any sign of the stock becoming exhausted.

People are naturally interested in the childhood

of remarkable men ; and shrewd observers, like
John Foster, are glad to recover, so far as recovery
is possible, those early mind impressions which
came and went like fleeting clouds in the fresh
spring-time of life's opening days.   Our first impressions of the world are for the most part lost ;
but on this account we value more highly than
we should the fragments which remain.   If he
had not himself narrated the fact, who could have
supposed that Mr. Spurgeon was ever fascinated
with the exciting sport of the hunting-field ?   Yet
so it was ; the dogs, the horses, the horn-blowing,
the riders in red coats, constituted a picturesque
paraphernalia which had irresistible charms.   Had
we, as inquisitive well-wishers, enquired in those
days what occupation Master Charles Haddon
Spurgeon would prefer as a life profession, the
reply would have come with smart readiness, " A
huntsman ! a huntsman ! "   Well may the man
exclaim as he looks back on such childish preferences, " A fine profession truly ! " but then
there is the unvarnished fact, as a child he "always
felt a natural taste for that sort of business."
Whenever the hounds were descried, they were
invariably followed at highest speed over fields,
hedges, and ditches, regardless of hazard.   The
indulgence of this propensity once cost dear ;
for, executing a market commission, the contents

of the basket—rice, mustard, etc.—were shaken together into " one awful mess." As anecdotes, such things are interesting contributions ; but as anecdotes merely they would never be told by Mr. Spurgeon. Everything must point a moral or serve as an illustration to clinch a religious truth. The childish predilection for field sports warns young men not to be too readily drawn into the Christian ministry by outward things, and thus resemble children who are captivated by the holiday trappings of sportsmen. The adventure likewise shows the value of a clear arrangement of ideas. Due care should be exercised so that good things are not heaped together " all in a muddle." It is obvious that " people will not drink your mustardy tea, nor will they enjoy muddled-up sermons, in which you cannot tell head from tail, because they have neither, but are like Mr. Bright's Skye terrier, whose head and tail were both alike."

Happy is the child to whom the season of school discipline comes with pleasures which are remembered with satisfaction in after life. Mr. Spurgeon met with good masters, and he drank in their teaching until he became himself a tutor with pupils taller than himself ; Colchester, Maidstone, and Newmarket all being associated with those early days. In connection with Colchester we once heard him relate this characteristic anecdote. On a certain very cold morning the tutor, without design, so arranged the class that the lower boys sat in proximity to the school stove, the comforting glow of which it was hardly worth while to surrender for the passing honours of priority. After he had asked sundry questions with unsatisfactory results, the schoolmaster suddenly, as he thought, discovered in the genial fire the one cause of Master Spurgeon's unusual dulness. The order was accordingly instantly given to wheel round, the head, instead of the bottom, of the class being now placed nearest the stove. The effect was exactly what the sagacious leader expected ; for when warmth as well as honour could be gained by proficiency, a few correct answers presently reinstated Master Spurgeon in his former place near the fire at the head of the column.

A child in whose susceptible heart the Old Adam so far predominated that he was carried off his head by the fascination of hunting would not in the natural course of things appear to everybody as a subject likely to succeed in the pulpit. A dame who was " as godly a Christian as ever breathed " thought that no good was ever likely to come of young Mr. Spurgeon's meddling with sacred things, and like a woman of conscience, if not of sense, she advised according to her light : she steadfastly dissuaded her young friend from assuming a calling for which it was so manifest that neither nature nor grace had fitted him. We cannot any of us afford to laugh at the judgment of this simple soul : for if it is hard to judge of a literary work in manuscript, how much more difficult is it to say what a preacher in embryo will achieve. If there were those living in the Puritan age who would have burned the manuscript of *The Pilgrim's Progress* to do God service, their descendants, in 1850, would act after the example of their fathers. The Fathers advised John Bunyan not to scandalise the church by printing a silly book ; the children, by shutting his mouth, would have made a tutor or a clerk of Mr. Spurgeon. In one case as in the other, a better judgment prevailed. It is, nevertheless, the Pastor's opinion that the young should show a deference to the counsel of their superiors in age and experience. The first sermon from the text, ,"Unto you, therefore, which believe He is precious," was preached unexpectedly and without preparation, and the work has ever since continued.

Probably Mr. Spurgeon has preached a greater number of sermons than any other living pastor of the same age ; and hence we are prepared for the admission that, all along, he has been careful of his throat. His advice to all public speakers is to discard once and for ever " horehound, ipecacuanha, or any of the ten thousand emollient compounds." His experience has taught him that for the voice there is nothing like astringents. When he removed from New Park Street to Exeter Hall he discovered that his voice was none too strong for a place so difficult to speak in ; but he found relief in Chili vinegar mixed with water, which he sipped occasionally during the service. He still finds a panacea in beef-tea " as strong with pepper as can be borne."

A preacher of such varied experience will necessarily have met with various entertaining adventures in connection with the business of choosing a text ; and Mr. Spurgeon ingenuously confesses that he is " an odd man." While residing at Cambridge, in the days of his village preaching, he on one occasion vainly endeavoured to collect his thoughts for a sermon, which had to be given in the evening. Do what he would " the right text" could not be found. After remaining some time in a somewhat anxious condition he happened to walk to the window, when on the roof of a house opposite were seen a company of vindictive sparrows worrying a solitary canary, which had been unfortunate enough to escape from its cage. After looking for a few moments,

the words of Jeremiah xii. 9 stole into his mind :
" Mine heritage is unto me as a speckled bird,
the birds round about are against me." "The
text was sent to. me," says the preacher, " and if
the ravens did not bring it, certainly the sparrows
did." Why do not the birds, or other agents in
nature, more often than they do bring our teachers
their texts ? Because all have not the eye to
utilize what they see. After he had seen the
sparrows and their victim, Mr. Spurgeon "walked
off with the greatest possible composure ; . . .
and preached upon the peculiar people and the
persecutions of their enemies."

While Mr. Spurgeon held the pastorate of
Waterbeach the inconvenient, old-fashioned custom
of holding three services on the Sabbath was still
in vogue. This usage, now in a great measure
obsolete, was one which a young pastor would not
find reason to admire ; for, leaving out of the
question the extra labour imposed, " roast beef
and pudding lie heavy on the hearers' souls, and
the preacher himself is deadened while digestion
claims the mastery of the hour." On a certain
Sabbath, during the happy days of youth, all went
well at morning service, and at dinner the preacher
ate sparingly, in order that he might wear well
through the afternoon. The sermon had been
thought out beforehand, without the aid of ink and

paper ; but in the hour of need, when the people were fast assembling in the meeting-house, the train of ideas suddenly vanished, leaving a dark vacuum, which occasioned some commendable trepidation in the mind. The fact was related to the farmer in whose house the dinner had been served ; but not having to preach himself that hospitable worthy made light of the mischief. It is all very well for farmers to say, " Oh! never mind, you will be sure to have a good word for us," and so on ; but such commonplaces are only cold comfort, and they do not point a way out of the difficulty. Just while the two were conversing a piece of wood, blazing and smoking, fell from the fire. Here was the missing link. " Here was a text, an illustration, and a leading thought as a nest-egg for more." The hearts of one or two were reached on that afternoon.

The above are interesting examples of their kind ; but a more extraordinary instance of a change of text having taken place, and not through any mishap, once occurred in the chapel at New Park Street on a Sunday evening. The preliminary parts of the service passed off in the usual manner ; the Bible was opened at the text selected and previously studied, when another passage hard by not only attracted attention, but seemed to spring up " like a lion from the thicket." The preacher tells us that he was " in a strait betwixt two." In imagination he seemed to listen to a dispute between the rivals; and when one pulled importunately at his skirts the other answered, " No, no, you must preach from me." The new comer had its way, and the first and second heads were proceeded with while the third head had not yet suggested itself. Immediately after the second division was closed the gas went out, and as the chapel was crowded with people the danger was considerable. The people were providentially saved from panic by hearing Mr. Spurgeon's voice, and the assurance that he could speak to them as well in the dark as the light. Two persons were reached and converted on that evening. " I cast myself upon God," says the preacher, " and His arrangements quenched the light at the proper time for me."

In his time Mr. Spurgeon has encountered many interesting specimens of the species called eccentric people. An uneducated genius in the pulpit has always something for the observant hearer in the pew. One of these persons referred to was a worthy who could found a sermon on such a text as " The night hawk, the owl, and the cuckoo." The text was, of course, ingeniously selected, but where were the divisions? Divisions? The birds had a head a-piece, and after wringing their necks

7

there they were.   The hawk was a sly rogue,
the owl was a drunkard who was most lively at
night, the cuckoo was one who harped on the
notes and sucked the eggs of others.   And yet
because the matter corresponded with the quaint
instrument it " did not seem at all remarkable
or odd."   This man was a godly rustic who was
great at spiritualizing ; and though long since
laid in the grave his memory lives in " Lectures
to my Students."

Pastors should cultivate the art of conversation,
they should be masters of the knack of turning to
profitable account the thousand and one every-day
incidents of ordinary life.   This was illustrated
by an adventure on Clapham Common some years
ago.   A common porter was pushing along a
large truck, and in the middle of the commodious
carriage lay a small parcel, perhaps looking more
diminutive than it really was by contrast.   " It
looks odd to see so large a truck for so small
a load," remarked Mr. Spurgeon.   " Yes, sir, it
is a very odd thing," quickly replied the man ;
" but do you know I've met with an odder thing
than that this blessed day.   I've been about
working and sweating all this 'ere blessed day,
and till now I haven't met with a gentleman
that looked as if he'd give me a pint of beer, till
I saw you."   What was the result of this deli-

cately-worded appeal we are not informed ; but
the ready earnestness with which the man sought
to turn the occasion to profit carried home a lesson
such as the interrogator was not slow to learn.
The opinion may be hazarded, however, that
in this instance the natural acuteness of the im-
portunate porter was overrated. From what we
know of the working classes of London we dare
affirm that there are hundreds who would have
manifested a corresponding smartness, the wit
and the repartee being second-hand, and thus
common property. Working men often speak
with great ease and drollery ; but then the witticisms thus admirably rendered may have existed
for generations.

Interested as we may be in all that we know
about Mr. Spurgeon's habits of study, ministers
and public speakers would do well to give some
extra attention to what he says concerning his
own efficiency in extempore speech, how he
acquired and how he sustains the coveted art.
The too common notion is that when a man
does anything remarkably well he does it without
taking trouble ; but the experience of real life
dispels such an illusion. It is through incessant
hard work alone that men succeed, and are able
to maintain their prestige when they have worked
their way to the front. This is strictly true of

Mr. Spurgeon ; for he has worked as hard as any man in England. In one sense, unfortunately, the position occupied by such a man is not without its drawbacks. The ceaseless pressure of work does not allow of the popular minister enjoying life like other people. Holidays are always scarce ; he may even be precluded from walking round his garden once in a week. He has a gift, and to maintain his standing the practice which is said to " make perfect" must be sustained.

As regards the manner of working, Mr. Spurgeon thinks it unsafe for those who retain their powers unimpaired to indulge in sticks, crutches, or spectacles. The preacher above every man should be self-reliant, and keep his natural faculties bright with constant service. Mr. Spurgeon's experience proves that those who would excel as extempore preachers must trust to memory and not to notes. Only make your notes a few lines longer this Sunday, and soon you will " require them longer still." He goes further, and assures us that if there is an increased trust in the pre-arrangements of memory, it is naturally followed by "a direct craving, and even an increased necessity for pre-composition." If the art of speaking well be encompassed with so many difficulties, which even a Spurgeon must

overcome, the lessons of his experience speak
to all.

To a public speaker a liberal supply of fresh
air is of vital importance, and this is especially
the case with the Pastor of the Tabernacle.
Occasionally, in the middle of a service, he will
ask for *more air*, and he counsels all pastors not
to be afraid of opening their chapel windows,
because " the next best thing to the grace of God
for a preacher is oxygen." He will not tolerate
having comfort in breathing sacrificed to architec-
ture ; and soon after settling at New Park Street
the officials found out to their cost the predilections of the Pastor. There was a window in the
chapel whose iron bars would not allow of its
being opened, and, after repeated suggestions had
been vainly made that a glazier should take out
the panes, they were one morning found to be
broken. The Pastor suggested that a reward of
£5 should be offered, and that the money should
be given as a testimonial to the offender ; and,
although he never informed, he went so far as
to confess that he had walked with the stick
which let the oxygen into a stifling structure.

A considerable weight of responsibility once
devolved on those who kept Mr. Spurgeon's
vestry-door, which after every service was surrounded with a goodly array of persons, one and

all having wants or whims to be satisfied. From time to time many "characters" appeared in the throng. Women with wild fancies, men with some chronic trouble weighing them down, or others who had visionary projects they would talk about to a sympathetic friend, might there have been encountered. Now and then the fire of insanity was to be detected in the eye of a new comer, and the arm of the sentinel deacon would be raised to hinder the ingress of a doubtful character. Among the more extraordinary specimens were found those who applied for admission to the Pastors' College. The college is Mr. Spurgeon's best-loved institution ; and it is generally known that candidates for the ministry may reckon on receiving patient attention. There are, of course, bold pretenders who come forward to turn liberty into licence, and to take advantage of good nature. One such was a young man whose face " looked like the title-page to a whole volume of conceit and deceit." The man had enough assurance for a hundred adventurers, and because his case was so remarkable he wanted to be admitted at once. His private opinion was that his attainments were immense, and that no such application had ever been received before. He testified that he had thoroughly explored the field of ancient and modern literature, while his preaching was exceptionally eloquent. When his application was declined, this upstart retired with dignity, supposing that an " unusual genius " and a " gigantic mind " showed the cause of failure.

Some references should be made to Mr. Spurgeon's editorial troubles, and to the offence which is necessarily given in some quarters through strict adherence to principle. All editors receive manuscripts of the most extraordinary description. A journalist once remarked that all persons suppose themselves to be competent writers, and the general experience of editors teaches that the assertion is not very wide of the truth. The absence of talent and education never damps the ardour of literary aspirants, whose sole ambition is to secure the honours of appearing in print. Who shall estimate the amazing amount of doggerel with which editors and publishers are still pestered ? The plague is a cross to bear, and shows signs of increase rather than of diminution. Although *cacoethes scribendi* may be a prevalent and incurable disease, we believe that general readers have little conception of the extent to which it prevails. There appears to be no class without its writers, or without those who suppose themselves to be capable of handling the quill.

As an editor, Mr. Spurgeon's adventures are
sure to be singular, proportionately with the
eminence of his position. Because his name is
known to everybody, the eccentric will not be
wanting in endeavours to take him into their
confidence. The poets are always a source of
trouble ; for not only do the doggerel traffickers
claim attention, a batch of rhymes was once
received from one who claimed to be divinely
inspired by the Holy Spirit ! Instead of being
inspired, however, all the pieces bore the mark
of imposture ; and did so because the editor's
shelves could " show many poems as much
superior to these pretended inspirations as angels
are to blue-bottles." What fool is to be compared with your " inspired " fool ?

Mr. Spurgeon is very partial to open-air
preaching, and in his lectures on that subject
gives many interesting incidents from his own
experience. His favourite pitch is the front of
" a rising ground, or an open spot bounded at
some little distance by a wall." Mr. Duncan's
garden at Benmore is a favourite site—" a level
sweep of lawn, backed by rising terraces, covered
with fir-trees." He also tells us of " a grand
cathedral " once provided for his accommodation
in Oxfordshire. " The remains of it are still
called Spurgeon's Tabernacle, and may be seen

near Minster Lovell, in the form of a quadrilateral of oaks. Originally it was the *beau ideal* of a preaching place, for it was a cleared spot in the thick forest of Wychwood, and was reached by roads cut through the dense underwood. I shall never forget those 'alleys green,' and the verdant walls which shut them in. When you reached the inner temple it consisted of a large square, out of which the underwood and smaller trees had been cut away, while a sufficient number of young oaks had been left to rise to a considerable height, and then overshadow us with their branches." He once preached in the time of haymaking from the appropriate text, " He shall come down like rain upon the mown grass, as showers that water the earth," but during the sermon a storm of rain passed over the ground. His general advice to open-air preachers is all valuable. Certain trees are to be avoided on account of their " rustling sound." The sun must not be directly in the speaker's face ; nor are they to attempt to preach "against the wind."

Such is a selection of personal reminiscences collected from his own works, which a future biographer of Mr. Spurgeon will be able to utilize. I could easily add other anecdotes which have not appeared in print ; but the insertion of these would unduly lengthen this chapter. I will, how-

ever, give one that comes from a trustworthy
friend concerning an English judge, now dead,
but who in his lifetime was very generally
esteemed, and who was deacon of a congregation
in London, a member of the Baptist denomination,
and, therefore, well acquainted with Mr. Spurgeon.
When out of court, or when in the ante-rooms,
both the justice and his learned associates converse familiarly among themselves, so that on one
occasion the Pastor of the Metropolitan Tabernacle became the topic of the hour. Of course
differences of opinion were freely expressed ; and
it is possible the brilliant coterie were a little
surprised on hearing from their friend the judge
that they should have an opportunity of deciding
for themselves the merits of the case, as he
intended to invite all of them, and also Mr.
Spurgeon, to a friendly dinner. "Do you mean it?"
cried the lawyers, in expectant tones. "Yes."
"Then agreed!" The bargain being thus con-
cluded, the worthy justice fulfilled to the letter
his part of the contract. Mr. Spurgeon accepted
the invitation, knowing nothing of the previous
arrangements ; and, as Dr. Johnson would have
said, the time passed well with some "good talk."
When the judge and counsel next met in the
robing room, the exceedingly hearty manner in
which the latter expressed their thanks showed

that they were not speaking in the dialect of mere compliment. Mr. Spurgeon was all that he was said to be, or even more ; and all confessed how well they had been entertained. The confession went even further ; they acknowledged that they had conspired together to test his knowledge by arranging beforehand a number of questions, and the answers received surpassed expectation. In point of fact, Mr. Spurgeon's table-talk is in itself good fare ; and hence we are well able to estimate the quality of the banquet which the lawyers enjoyed, and acknowledged with a *bonhomie* characteristic of their order when out of court. Indeed, this table-talk is too good to be lost, but there are difficulties in the way of its collection ; for, as I remarked at the outset, " what the Pastor has been heard to threaten he will do, should he ever be approached by a first cousin of Johnson's biographer, may well intimidate the boldest member of that inquisitive tribe."

On December 1st, 1880, Mr. Spurgeon gave some reminiscences of his earlier days which may very properly close the present chapter :—*

After thanking his people " from the bottom

---

* The report of what the Pastor said on this interesting occasion is that which appeared at the time in *The Christian World.*

of his soul" for the hearty way in which they
had ever worked with him, Mr. Spurgeon said
he was afraid they were getting old together.
Speaking for himself, however, he felt young
about the head, but quite old down below. His
life had been specially interesting, and he was
not likely to grow tired of it. He verily believed
that had he the power of a novelist he could
produce a three-volume novel from the events
of any one day of his life, so singularly had that
life been crowded with interesting incidents.
Indeed, if he were ever dull, it must be from
something within, for he could not get gloomy
from the outside. He had promised to tell them
a few stories of things he could recollect ; and a
face he saw before him reminded him of a visit
he once paid to Tring. He was regarded as
being too *high* for one chapel there, too *low* for
another, but in a third he was permitted to preach.
The pastor of this chapel was in receipt of only
fifteen shillings a-week, and Mr. Spurgeon had
some misgivings about drinking the poor man's
tea. During the meal he noticed that his host
wore a very shiny alpaca coat. At the close of
the sermon Mr. Spurgeon said, addressing the
congregation—" Now I have preached my best
to you. ' Freely ye have received, freely give.'
The minister of this place looks as if he wants

a new suit of clothes. I will give half-a-sovereign, my friend down below will do the same, and plates will be held at the doors for your contributions." The effort was successful. After the service the poor pastor, addressing Mr. Spurgeon, observed that ever since he became a minister of Jesus Christ his Master always sent him his livery, and he was beginning to wonder where the next would come from. The same day and in the same place Mr. Spurgeon addressed a gathering of children, and was subsequently severely taken to task by some good men for telling the little ones that God heard his prayers before he was converted. The grave men gathered around, exclaiming that the prayers of a sinner were an abomination to the Lord. The victory was, however, won by an old woman in a red cloak. " What are you battling with this young man about ? " she inquired, squeezing herself into the circle. " What do *you* know about the Scriptures ? You say God does not hear the prayers of unconverted people, why, have you never read that He heareth the young ravens when they cry ? and there is no grace in them. If God hears the cry of the ravens, don't you think He will hear the cry of a man made in His own image !" The objectors suddenly vanished, and Mr. Spurgeon walked away with the old lady.

His earliest recollections, Mr. Spurgeon went on to say, gathered around his grandfather, who was for sixty-four years pastor of a congregation at Stambourne, in Essex, and at the age of eighty-eight was wont to rub his knee and complain that rheumatism was shortening his days. Mr. Spurgeon acknowledged that he owed a great deal to the teaching of his early youth. When a boy, and while staying at his grandfather's house, he met the Rev. Richard Knill, the missionary, who would take him into an arbour and pray with him. On one occasion Mr. Knill lifted him on to his knee, and said that he felt persuaded the child would grow up to preach the Gospel to more people than any man living, and that he would one day preach in Rowland Hill's Chapel. Mr. Knill gave him sixpence, in return for which he was to learn the hymn, " God moves in a mysterious way," and at the same time extracted the promise from little Spurgeon that he would have this hymn sung when he occupied Rowland Hill's pulpit. On coming to London the preacher was taken ill, and Mr. Spurgeon was asked to take the service in Surrey Chapel. He did so, and redeemed his promise by letting the congregation sing the hymn suggested by Mr. Knill. Strange things came about in the working of God's providence. It was through Mr. Knill daring to preach in a theatre, that led Mr. Spurgeon to conduct services in the Surrey Music Hall. He became a Baptist through reading the New Testament, especially in the Greek, and was strengthened in his resolve by a perusal of the Church of England Catechism. He was baptised at the age of fifteen in a river. Two women, who were immersed at the same time, desired him to lead them into the water; but he was such a timid, trembling creature that he needed all the strength he possessed for himself. But his timidity was washed away. It floated down the river into the sea, and must have been devoured by the fishes, for he had never felt anything of the kind since. Baptism also loosed his tongue, and from that day it had never been quiet. When Mr. Spurgeon became pastor of the church of Waterbeach they held their baptisms in a neighbouring river. There was to be a baptism one day, and it was raining "cats and dogs." The service was to be undertaken by Mr. Elvin, a man of enormous size, who said he must decline, for if he got wet through there was not a waist-coat within forty miles that would fit him. One day when Mr. Elvin was preaching for Mr. Spurgeon at Park Street, an old lady put her head in at the door, and, perceiving Mr. Elvin, withdrew, remarking that "no good could

possibly come from a man who had so much of
the flesh." Mr. Spurgeon went on to remark that
he recollected most distinctly hearing Mr. Jay
preach at Cambridge. The text was, " Ever let
your conversation be as becometh the Gospel of
Christ." And he remembered with what dignity
he preached, and yet how simply. Ladies, Mr.
Jay said, in the course of his sermon, were sometimes charged with dressing too costly. He did
not know much about it himself, but if they told
him what their income was he would tell them
how many yards of ribbon they could afford.
His recollections of Mr. Jay were such as he
would not like to lose.

On another occasion he made a journey to
Birmingham to hear John Angell James, for he
was most anxious to be able to say that he had
heard Jay and James. Mr. James's text was, " Ye
are complete in Him." And what a delicious
sermon it was! Years afterwards, on being in
Mr. James's company, Mr. Spurgeon told him that
he went all the way to Birmingham to hear him
preach. On his mentioning the text, Mr. James
replied, " Ah! that was a Calvinistic sermon.
You would get on with that, but you would not
get on with me always." Dr. Brock, when dining
with Mr. James on one occasion, asked him if he
recollected preaching at a certain place for two

hours. " I do," replied Mr. James, " but the clock
did not indicate it." " No," said Dr. Brock ; " I
was in the gallery, and stopped the clock whenever I liked, and thus made you preach for two
hours instead of three-quarters of an hour."
At this Mr. James observed, " Mr. Brock, you
always were at your fun, and I daresay you
would do the same again." " But I wouldn't,"
retorted Dr. Brock, to the great surprise of Mr.
James, who expected the Doctor would still be
desirous of hearing a sermon from him extending
over two hours at least. Dr. Brock's tone suggested pretty plainly that if he happened to be
a listener again, he would rather make the hands
travel unusually quick in the orthodox direction.

When Mr. Spurgeon commenced preaching at
Waterbeach he was sixteen years old. The
people could do but very little for his support ;
hence he also filled the post of an usher at
Cambridge. After a time he gave the latter
occupation up, and trusted to the generosity of
his people, who raised about £45 a-year for him.
Out of this he paid twelve shillings a-week for
two rooms, and his congregation did for him what
he wished country congregations generally would
do for their pastors. Whenever they went to
Cambridge they carried him vegetables, and any
quantity of loaves of bread, and at no time did any

member of his flock kill a pig without his receiving some portion of it. Once young Spurgeon was invited to preach for Mr. Sutton, who, on perceiving the youth for the first time on his arrival, exclaimed, " You can't preach. What is the world coming to ? A parcel of boys preaching who have not got their mothers' milk out of their mouths ! " Mr. Sutton was a quaint old man, who, after being a shepherd of sheep for forty years, became shepherd of men for a similar period, and was wont to remark that his second flock " was a deal more sheepish than the first."

Mr. Spurgeon went on to observe that his (Mr. Spurgeon's) acquaintance had been most varied and extensive. He had enjoyed the friendship of most of the noblest persons that had passed over the history of his own time. He just happened to have the least possible connection with Christmas Evans, having found his widow nearly starving, and it was his great joy to support her till she died. A friend, now gone, however, on hearing of it, insisted upon having shares in the pleasurable undertaking. Mr. Spurgeon remarked that if he had not washed the feet of Christmas Evans, he had done what he could for any relic there was left of him.

Then he enjoyed, too, the most intimate friendship of Daubigné, author of the " History of the

Reformation," who once gave an address at the Tabernacle. Mr. Spurgeon also preached for Daubigné on the continent, and the same day occupied Calvin's old pulpit. In the evening he met two hundred of the greatest preachers of Switzerland, and before departing, one after the other kissed him on both cheeks. It was his pleasure to have the personal friendship of Mr. Sherman, also that of Dr. Hamilton, whom it was always a real joy to meet in his own home. Then he well knew glorious old Tom Guthrie. "What a man he was to be with!" said Mr. Spurgeon. "And he could tell a story or two. When we were together we were happy." And Dr. Candlish it was his delight to be acquainted with. He well recollected addressing the General Assembly of the Free Church of Scotland, and Dr. Candlish was all over the place—now in the gallery, now to the moderator's right, now to his left. Dr. Candlish was made of quicksilver, and, though his body was not very large, it seemed to partake of the quicksilver of his nature. Mr. Spurgeon regarded Candlish as one of the greatest men of modern times. And then he knew Arnot, and should not soon forget the good old man. "All honour to these men," added Mr. Spurgeon. "They did not come to England, but they did exceedingly well in Scotland, where they were

burning and shining lights." He owed much to
the Scotch, for when his Tabernacle was being
built, a considerable portion of the money came
from the North. Whenever he went to Scotland
—it was not " Blue-bonnets over the Border," but
wide-awake over the Border—he came back loaded
with money. He just passed over the skirts of
the Claytons, and everybody who lived in Wal-
worth recollected what gentlemen the Claytons
were. Without a doubt they were the most
gentlemanly race of preachers that ever lived.
Mr. Spurgeon did not lament that such dignified
brethren had passed away, though they did good
in their day. He had been told that souls were
saved by the white bibs ministers wore. Then
John Howard Hinton had a good word for him
when very few had anything to say in his favour.
He called in at the Tabernacle one day, and said
to Mr. Olney, Mr. Spurgeon's senior deacon,
" Take care of that young man ; he is an old
Puritan bound in morocco." " But I maintain,"
added Mr. Spurgeon, " that I am bound in calf,
for I belong to Essex." Then that good old Dr.
Campbell, editor of the *British Banner*, was a very
dear friend of his. Whenever he went to preach
for Dr. Campbell he had always to take his wife
and boys with him. When writing to invite them
Dr. Campbell would say, "Our cat has had kittens

on purpose for the boys to play with." And the
day before their arrival the good old man would
be out buying toy horses and carts for the juvenile
Spurgeons. This showed that while he was a
stern man he stooped down to do a kindly action,
and took a pleasure in delighting children. Dr.
Binney once went to hear Mr. Spurgeon, and
remarked of the sermon in the presence of some
of the preacher's friends—" It is an insult to God
and man. I never heard such a thing." Twenty
years afterwards Dr. Binney visited the Pastors'
College and related the incident, observing, "Well,
you know, your minister has so much improved
since those days. I denounced him then most
heartily, and even refused to preach where he
preached, but I very soon found out my mistake."
"And the grand, great man," added Mr. Spurgeon,
" was perhaps right in his first observation ! "
After mentioning a few other incidents, Mr.
Spurgeon brought his chat to a close, promising
to resume it on a future occasion.

When Dr. Binney took exception to the style
of the young preacher, he was not so singular
in his prejudices as some might now be disposed
to think. In 1851, when Mr. Spurgeon commenced work, the world may not have been
unprepared to greet something new—to condone
some departure from the old and beaten ways ;

but it was hardly ready to welcome a preacher of such thorough originality, that he ignored time-honoured conventional pulpit fashions to follow methods of his own ; even his most uncompromising detractors did not attempt to deny that the preacher was original ; but the world did not find in such an admission a passport to its favour. This was partly accounted for by the fact, that in great measure people spoke and acted as their fathers had done before them. A Latinised rhetorical style was still regarded as eloquence ; and the "great" sermons of popular orators at important anniversaries were marvellous examples of painstaken elaboration. The success of Mr. Spurgeon meant a total change of fashion ; 'but the world does not change its ways at the bidding of a provincial youth without some growls and warm protests. Elderly people did not know that what they thought to be so proper was doomed to become obsolete ; and they could not be expected all at once to apprehend that the youth whom they accused of so many improprieties was really a reformer, such as the pulpit and the world had long wanted.

ANECDOTES, LETTERS, ANA, ETC.

" Gentlemen of the press have an eye to the amusement of their readers, and make selections of all the remarkable anecdotes, or odd sayings, used by a speaker, and when these are separated from their surroundings the result is anything but satisfactory. No man's speeches or lectures should be judged of by an ordinary newspaper summary, which in any case is a mere sketch, and in many instances is a vile caricature."—*Preface to Eccentric Preachers.*

V.

ANECDOTES, LETTERS, ANA, ETC.

TRUTH *versus* FICTION.

LIKE Rowland Hill and some other celebrated preachers of wit and wisdom, Mr. Spurgeon has had many apocryphal stories told about him, and the manner in which these piquant fictions are circulated is well illustrated by the following letter, which the Pastor received in the year 1883:—

"As I see that you are still occasionally put to the trouble of answering enquiries as to the truth of various anecdotes, etc., concerning yourself, I thought the following brief statement might interest you, or some of your numerous readers, if you think it well to publish it. About seventeen years ago I was for some time at a well-known health-resort on the south coast. At the *table d'hôte* I sat next to a young married lady, who was, alas! consumptive; and of that temperament which is so common in such cases, *très spirituelle,* and very learned and accomplished. You may be sure she never lacked auditors for her lively conversation. At dessert one day she was 'telling stories,' in the juvenile and literal sense of the phrase, about yourself. I let her go on for some time, until I thought the fun was getting a little too fast; and then I said, ' I hope, Mrs. ——, you do not believe the stories you are detailing, because I assure you I heard nearly all of them in my childhood, before Mr. Spurgeon was born, and that most of them were then attributed to Rowland Hill—doubtless with equal lack of authenticity.' She looked me calmly in the face, with a very comical expression, and replied, ' Oh, Mr. ——, we never ask whether such stories are true ; it is quite sufficient if we find them amusing.' ' Well,' I said, ' *so long as that is understood all round*, by all means keep on.' The poor, brilliant, thoughtless woman, and her husband also, have many years since passed away ; but she has many, many successors, who are without her wit, and not quite so good-humouredly candid as to their practice. If only you can get it ' understood all round,' that such folk really do not consider whether their ' anecdotes ' are true or not, it might save you some trouble." In reference to this, Mr. Spurgeon himself remarked : " This is quite true, but it is a pity that people should lie in jest. The lady

was let off very easily. Our friend has touched
the root of the matter. It is not malice, but the
passion for amusement, which creates the trade in
falsehood, which never seems to decline."

CLAPHAM AND WESTWOOD.

The *North British Daily Mail* once remarked
that those who have visited Mr. Spurgeon at his
home in Nightingale Lane, from which he lately
removed to Norwood, will recollect having seen in
the pleasant garden the old pulpit stairs that were
used at the great preacher's first London chapel—
the old meeting-house in New Park Street, where
he was preceded as pastor by a long line of
worthy ministers—Dr. Gill, the learned Hebraist;
Dr. Rippon, the editor of the old Baptist Hymn-
book; Dr. Joseph Angus, the Bible Reviser,
and Mr. Smith, of Cheltenham. When the chapel
was sold Mr. Spurgeon removed the pulpit stairs
to his garden, and fixed them to the trunk of a
huge willow tree. "Here," says Mr. Spurgeon,
"the observer can see those very rails down which
we did *not* slide to illustrate backsliding, and he
may be sure of that negative fact, because the
story was told of us when the pulpit was fixed in
the wall and the entrance was from behind; and
more than that, the same story was told of another
preacher before we were born." Mr. Spurgeon

has not taken the stairs with him to his new home at Norwood. He has left them attached to the great willow in Nightingale Lane. " The purchaser of our former abode," he says, " will preserve the staircase quite as carefully as we have done, and we hope his children will for years ascend by them to the pleasant seats, where they may in the summer sit and enjoy themselves beneath the willow's shade."

AT HOME AT WESTWOOD.

Before leaving England for America, Dr. Theodore Cuyler visited Mr. Spurgeon at his new home near the Crystal Palace, and in a letter to the New York *Evangelist* describes his villa as " a rural Paradise." " The great preacher," writes Dr. Cuyler, " with a jovial countenance, came out of his door with both hands outstretched to give us welcome. Saturday afternoon is his holiday. For an hour he conducted us over his delightful grounds and through his garden and conservatory, and then to a rustic arbour, where he entertained us with one of his racy talks which are as characteristic as his sermons. Mr. Spurgeon's study is a charming apartment opening out on his lawn ; the view extends for twelve miles to Epsom Downs. His parlour, too, is lined with elegant volumes. He showed us with great glee a portfolio of

caricatures of himself ; and then, by way of contrast, a series of translations of his sermons in
various foreign tongues. His comely wife—for a
long time a suffering invalid—presided at the
table with grace and sweetness. Their twin sons
have already entered the ministry, one in London
and the other now in New Zealand. It was six
o'clock on Saturday when we bade him 'good-
bye,' and he assured us that he had not yet
selected even the text for next day's discourses !
' I shall go down in the garden presently,' said he,
' and arrange my morning discourse and choose
a text for that in the evening : then to-morrow
afternoon, before preaching, I will make an outline
of the second one.' This has been his habit for
many years ; he never composes a sentence in
advance, and rarely spends over half-an-hour in
laying out the plan of a sermon. Constant study
fills his mental cask, and he has only to turn the
spigot and draw."

THE PASTOR AT PLYMOUTH.

While at the Baptist Union Meetings at
Plymouth in 1875, Mr. Spurgeon told the
following anecdotes :—

Unaired Drawing-rooms.—I was at a minister's
house the other day, and he said, looking at the
drawing-room, " Well, you see this drawing-room

looks a little seedy." I said that I did not think it did. " Well," he said, " my wife has a Bible-class here every Sunday, and she generally gets it once in the week. In my study I always have a young men's Bible-class on a Sunday afternoon." Oh! good friends, your houses were not meant to be half shut up as they are. When I call on some of my people, if they happen to be a little upper-crust, they put me up in the drawing-room in the winter even, when there has not been a fire there for three months, and I get the rheumatism, and I go out of the room saying to myself, " I wish to goodness those people would have a service there every week, for if they did that the room would be aired, and there would be an incidental blessing to me, and I do not doubt it would be so to them."

The Rose of Sharon.—I met the other day a lady who had lost the sense of taste and the sense of smell ; I had never met with a person before in that condition. The sweetest fragrance of a rose was lost upon her nostril, and the choicest delicacies had not the slightest flavour to her. It was a painful loss, in some measure ; but, oh ! what a wretch a man must be who has lost the power of smelling the fragrance of the Rose of Sharon, and lost his taste so that he does not perceive any sweetness in the fruit which came down from heaven, even Jesus Christ. I feel in a pitying mood as I look at you that do not love Him. Oh, what perverted tastes you have got! what strange judgments! for you love this painted Jezebel of a world ; you love this witch of sinful pleasure ; but my Lord, who is altogether lovely, who puts the angels in amazement every time they get a gaze upon Him—you do not love. Oh! what has happened to you ? What strange madness has come over you ?

The Newfoundland Dog.—I read in the " Guide to Kingsbridge" a pretty story about the Start Bay villages, where the Newfoundland dogs are kept to go out to sea to fetch in a rope. The story is that one of these dogs saw a child in the water and swam in and brought the child out. He could do that, and as he laid the child down on the sand it was nearly dead, and he licked its face to try and bring it round ; and when he found that his licking would not revive it, he went up to a village, and he caught hold of people's coats, till at last he induced some to come down and by their care the little flame of life in the child, which was almost extinct, was made to burn up again. As I read the story, I hoped to be something like that dog. I will go into the water after souls and try to bring them out ; and, if. I could, I would kiss them into life with loving words ; but as that is out of my power, I will. go and tug the skirts of Jesus, and ask Him to come and give them life, and raise them up, and I do not doubt that He will do so. That was a dog's work. Christians, do something more than dogs can do, or, at least, attempt to do as well. God grant you may ; and though you cannot quicken them into life, you can bring Jesus to them, and He can give them life and strength that they may be saved.

The Power of Kindness.——One day an old man shook me by the hand with a firm grasp, and he said, " Sir, one Sunday night you said, ' Every one of you do something to-night for Jesus such as you never did before.' Now," he said, " my son had been a great trouble to me. He was a very wicked youth indeed, and he had left me for some time, and he had brought himself to death's door by his ill habits. I had, therefore, given him enough to live upon ; but I thought to do nothing else. But that night," said he, " I went home and looked out of my larder the best things I had got, and I put them in a basket, and I sent them round to my son to tell him that I had forgiven him all, and that I had sent him a little something extra that night, and I meant to do it continually, and I hoped that he would get well. Now," said he, " I never could speak to him of religion till

I did that; and the next morning I went round and we were able to converse about the things of God, and he died with a comfortable hope; whereas, before, I had been afraid that he would die far from God."

The two following letters were also printed for the first time about sixteen years ago in my History of the Tabernacle Church. Of course they have been copied by others, so remarkable are they when read in connection with what has since happened.

"No. 60, Park Street, Cambridge,

"*January 27th*, 1854.

"My dear Sir,—I cannot help feeling intense gratification at the unanimity of the Church at New Park Street, in relation to their invitation to me. Had I been uncomfortable in my present situation, I should have felt unmixed pleasure at the prospect Providence seems to open up before me; but having a devoted and loving people, I feel I know not how.

"One thing I know, viz., that I must soon be severed from them by necessity, for they do not raise sufficient to maintain me in comfort. Had they done so, I should have turned a deaf ear to any request to leave them, at least for the present. But now my Heavenly Father drives me forth from this little Garden of Eden, and whilst I see that I must go out, I leave it with reluctance, and tremble to tread the unknown land before.

"When I first ventured to preach at Waterbeach, I only accepted an invitation for three months, on the

9

condition that, if in that time I should see good reason for leaving, or they, on their part, should wish for it, I should be at liberty to cease supplying, or they should have the same power to request me to do so before the expiration of the time.

"Now with regard to a six months' invitation from you, I have no objection to the length of time, but rather approve of the prudence of the Church in wishing to have one so young as myself on an extended period of probation.

"But I write after well weighing the matter, when I say positively that I cannot, I *dare* not, accept an unqualified invitation for so long a time. My objection is not to the length of the time of probation, but it ill becomes a youth to promise to preach to a London congregation so long until he knows *them* and they know *him*. I would engage to supply for three months of that time, and then, should the congregation fail or the Church disagree, I would reserve to myself liberty, without breach of engagement, to retire; and you would, on your part, have the right to dismiss me without seeming to treat me ill. Should I see no reason for so doing, and the Church still retain their wish for me, I can remain the other three months, either with or without the formality of a further invitation; but even during that time (the second three) I should not like to regard myself as a fixture, in case of ill success, but should only be a supply—liable to a fortnight's dismissal or resignation.

" Perhaps this is not business-like. I do not know, but this is the course I should prefer, if it would be agreeable to the Church. Enthusiasm and popularity are often the cracking of thorns and soon expire. I do not wish to be a hindrance if I cannot be a help.

" With regard to coming at *once*, I think I must

not. My own deacons just hint that I ought to finish the quarter here, though by *ought*, they mean simply, 'Pray do so if you can.' This would be too long a delay. I wish to help them until they can get supplies, which is only to be done with great difficulty, and as I have given you four Sabbaths, I hope you will allow me to give them four in return. I would give them the first and second Sabbath in February, and two more in a month or six weeks' time. I owe them much for their kindness, although they insist that the debt lies on their side. Some of them hope and almost pray that you may be tired in three months, so that I may be again sent back to them.

"Thus, my dear Sir, I have honestly poured out my heart to you. You are too kind. You will excuse me if I err, for I wish to do right to you, to my people, and to all, as being not mine own, but bought with a price.

"I respect the honesty and boldness of the small minority, and only wonder that the number was not greater. I pray God that if He does not see fit that I should remain with you, the majority may be quite as much the other way at the end of six months, so that I may never divide you into parties.

"Pecuniary matters I am well satisfied with. And now one thing is due to every minister, and I pray you to remind the Church of it, viz., that in private, as well as public, they must all earnestly wrestle in prayer to the God of our Lord Jesus Christ that I may be sustained in the great work.

"I am, with the best wishes for your health, and the greatest respect,

"Yours truly,

"C. H. Spurgeon.

"James Low, Esq."

"75, DOVER ROAD, BOROUGH,

"*April 28th,* 1854.

" *To the Baptist Church of Christ worshipping in New Park Street, Southwark.*

"DEARLY BELOVED IN CHRIST JESUS,—I have received your unanimous invitation as contained in a resolution passed by you on the 19th inst., desiring me to accept the pastorate among you.

" No lengthened reply is required ; there is but one answer to so loving and cordial an invitation, *I accept it.*

" I have not been perplexed as to what my reply should be, for many things constrain me thus to answer.

" I sought not to come to you, for I was the minister of an obscure but affectionate people ; I never solicited advancement. The first note of invitation from your deacons came quite unlooked for, and I trembled at the idea of preaching in London ; I could not understand how it had come about, and even now I am filled with astonishment at the wondrous Providence. I would wish to give myself into the hands of our covenant God, whose wisdom directs all things : He shall choose for me, and so far as I can judge this is His choice.

" I feel it to be a high honour to be the pastor of a people who can mention glorious names as my predecessors, and I entreat of you to remember me in prayer that I may realise the responsibility of my trust. Remember my youth and inexperience, pray that these may not hinder my usefulness. I trust also that the remembrance of these will lead you to forgive mistakes I may make, or unguarded words I may utter.

" Blessed be the name of the Most High ! if He has called me to this office, He will support me in it, otherwise how should a child, a youth, have the presumption thus to attempt a work which filled the heart and hands of Jesus ?

"Your kindness to me has been very great, and my heart is knit unto you. I fear not *your* steadfastness, I fear my own. The Gospel, I believe, enables me to venture great things, and by faith I venture this.

"I ask your co-operation in every good work; in visiting the sick, in bringing in enquirers, and in mutual edification.

"Oh that I may be no injury to you, but a lasting benefit! I have no more to say saving this, that if I have expressed myself in these few words in a manner unbecoming my youth and inexperience, you will not impute it to arrogance, but forgive my mistake.

"And now, commending you to our covenant God, the Triune Jehovah,

"I am, yours to serve in the Gospel,

"C. H. SPURGEON."

AT MENTONE.

It is very probable that the majority of friends who regularly, or occasionally, attend the services at the Metropolitan Tabernacle are quite unable to appreciate what a holiday means to a man in Mr. Spurgeon's position. To superficial observers the great chapel may seem to be little more than a popular preaching-station, which, indeed, it was represented to be some years ago by a well-known clergyman, now a bishop—a centre of evangelical teaching, of which neighbouring churches scarce knew the existence when the doors were closed and the gas was out. If this were all, the strain on the Pastor would nevertheless still be very heavy ; for even a genius in his work cannot preach three sermons a week of a high standard of excellence without being subjected to a wear and tear such as does not enter into the experience of more humble workers. As most persons know, however, the offices in the rear and beneath the Tabernacle are the headquarters of a large number of philanthropic agencies, some of which are of considerable magnitude, while all, in a greater or lesser degree, demand the Pastor's oversight. In the colportage department, in the general secretary's room, and elsewhere on the chapel premises, a goodly number of persons are regularly employed ; while at Westwood, two busy assistants, on either side of the large table in the study, have all that they can do to clear up each day's work as it comes. It is thus hardly to be wondered at that commenting and general literary work should appear to go only slowly forward to those who for years patiently waited for the concluding volume of *The Treasury of David.*

In Mr. Spurgeon's case there is supposed to be some connection between excessive suffering from rheumatism and too much work ; but if this is so, the invalid is probably paying the penalty exacted by the indiscretions of former days. That the ailment is hereditary we are well aware ; for the Puritan grandfather, who died at Stambourne in 1866, was wont to declare, when verging on ninety years of age, that rheumatism would certainly shorten his days. Still, all the suffering which has afflicted the family since Job Spurgeon lay as a prisoner in Chelmsford gaol for con-science' sake in the time of Charles II. can hardly have amounted to what the Pastor of the Metro-politan Tabernacle has endured in twenty years ; and probably the seeds of a good deal of this pain and weakness were sown when the youthful orator travelled up and down the country preaching a dozen sermons a week ; when, besides the usual inconveniences of the road, such as hasty meals and having to study in express trains, he incurred the more alarming risk of damp beds. It would seem that these well-meant indiscretions of the past are now causing some inconvenience.

As a holiday resort during our English winter and so-called boreal spring, Mentone has many charms ; but perhaps all the encomiums passed upon the picturesque Mediterranean nook have not been verified by the majority who have sought benefit from its sunshine and sea breezes. The climate, enjoyable as it must be when lemon-trees blossom in mid-winter, and flies sport in the sunshine, has not done so much for Mr. Spurgeon as was at first fondly anticipated by those who thought that the rheum might possibly be expelled from the system by genial climatic influences. The fact is, however, that even Mentone is not a perfect sanatorium : " Indeed," says Dr. Benet, " I question whether in the South of Europe, in winter, it is not as difficult to keep free from rheumatic pains as it is in the north." He then goes on to tell how the painful malady exists in all southern climes, including even the Sahara Desert, adding that "the Bedouin Arabs, with the thermometer at 80° or 90° in the daytime, swathe themselves up in woollen garments and woollen cloaks, for rheumatism is their enemy as well as ours." It is plain that, in Mr. Spurgeon's case, a more moderated strain on the mental faculties would effect far more than change of climate.

Social life in a small holiday community like that of Mentone has its sombre aspects, on account of the number of invalids who arrive, never to return to their homes. French consumptives succumb before winter has well begun ; and though they sometimes linger longer, the English who are afflicted in a similar manner surely follow one by one. These losses cast a shade over the whole of the foreign settlement, because, as Dr. Benet says, "the departed have endeared themselves to the survivors ; they have lived amongst them, they have shared their joys, their sorrows, their exile feeling." The advent of the magnificent southern spring in March may do something towards exhilarating the more ordinary visitors, however ; for it is there that the sun asserts a power which no temporary return of winter will challenge, when in the vales, and on the heights alike, wild flowers blossom with a beauty and a profusion which astonish those who look upon the classic shores of the Mediterranean for the first time.

In this favoured region, and on the verge of such a spring as the ancient classic poets praised in their verse, Mr. Spurgeon will secure that rest and quiet which will do more for him than medicine or the physician's art. His own people have sometimes requested that he will remain away for an extended period, and while so doing they also give a guarantee that all will do their best to keep the varied machinery at home in good working order. On some occasions the subscriptions have shown a tendency to fall off when the Pastor has been away, and this has in some measure marred his pleasure, if it has not actually retarded his recovery. If friends near and far away really desire to contribute to

Mr. Spurgeon's holiday, they will ever do so most effectively by keeping the Orphanage, the College, the Colportage, and other agencies well supplied while he is away. The mill is now in all its parts so large an affair, that more grist than ever is needed to keep it going; and when symptoms of falling off betray themselves, none suffer so keenly as the chief overseer himself, on whom the responsibility mainly rests of keeping up the supplies.

On Going to America.

He always set his face against going to America; but during the summer of 1876 the subject was revived by the appearance of a paragraph in *The Boston Globe* to the effect that the much-talked-about visit to the United States was really coming off. On seeing this notice the managers of the Redpath Lyceum Bureau wrote one more application thus :—

"Boston, Mass., *June 22nd,* 1876.

"Dear Sir,—Is the above paragraph true? We have tried so long and so hard for many years to secure you that we thought it impossible, and long since gave up all hope. We are the exclusive agents of all the leading lecturers in America. We will give you 1,000 dollars in gold for every lecture you deliver in America, and pay all your expenses to and from your home, and place you under the most popular auspices in the country. Will you come?"

To this invitation Mr. Spurgeon returned the following reply:

"CLAPHAM, LONDON, ENGLAND, *July 6th*.

"GENTLEMEN,—I cannot imagine how such a paragraph should appear in your papers, except by deliberate invention of a hard-up editor, for I never had any idea of leaving home for America for some time to come. As I said to you before, if I could come, I am not a lecturer, nor would I receive money for preaching."

"A HOLIDAY (?)."

After the first Sunday in August 1876 he visited Scotland, accompanied by his two sons, for the purpose of enjoying some yachting among the Western Islands or Hebrides. He was for the time being the guest of Mr. Duncan of Benmore. On the Sunday after his arrival he preached at Scone, in the open air, to five thousand persons, seats being provided for the ladies. In consequence of these services the neighbouring sanctuaries were closed. In the morning sermon he spoke of the hatred which separated sects between whom there were but few points of difference, and he warned the Scotch to take care that this was not the case with them. Even a microscope could not discover any material difference between certain of the sects. In the evening he said he would talk in a more familiar strain. He directly addressed those who had heard more sermons than they could count. They had listened to waggon-loads, they were smoked in sermons, and yet were still unconverted. Some people at the Tabernacle, though very few, had heard the Gospel for twenty years and were not caught yet, and it was to be feared they never would be. They were like india-rubber—no matter how often you depressed it, the substance returned to its original form.

On the following Sabbath he preached again at Kileret to many thousands, who assembled on the hill-side which overlooks the Firth of Clyde. On this occasion the northerners appear to have been surprised at the extraordinary power and clearness of his magnificent voice.

Concerning this so-called " holiday," he sent a brief note to a gentleman at Glasgow, and addressed from Carlisle on his way home :—

" DEAR FRIEND,—I have returned to England. I had eleven clear week-days in Scotland, and was asked to preach more than fifty times. *That* when I came for rest—and in a Christian country, too ! ' A merciful man,' etc. God speed you.—Yours truly, C. H. SPURGEON."

IN SCOTLAND IN 1878.

The visit to the North was this year deferred through various causes, and when the trip was

actually undertaken he was so worried to preach
that he did not derive the good from the change
he might otherwise have done. A correspondent
of *The Baptist* thus wrote respecting this visit :—

" Mr. Spurgeon arrived in the Bay of Rothesay, on
Saturday, the 27th July, in Mr. Duncan's fine yacht.
The celebrated preacher sailed from Oban to Campbelltown, passing the Mull of Kintyre. Sailing from
Campbelltown, he passed round a considerable part of
the Island of Arran. The scenery along Arran is most
delightful. He passed through the far-famed Kyles of
Bute. The Kyles narrow and broaden, and narrow and
broaden again. The whole atmosphere is of arcadian
seclusion. Tighnabruaich nestles down below the
hills, the houses rising a little from the shore only to
be half hidden in the surrounding foliage. The very
narrowness of the water and the consequent closeness
of the land on either side are themselves portions of
the fascinations exercised by the place. Here the
scenery is of the most charming description. The
waterway is so narrow that you can see the land on
either side distinctly, and even count the number of
the hills. Leaving the Kyles, Rothesay, the charming
capital of Bute, is reached, noted for its aquarium.
Arrived in Rothesay Bay, Mr. Spurgeon landed for a
drive in the island, when, coming down a declivity,
the horse in the machine ran away, and great danger
was apprehended; but, fortunately, a gentleman caught
the frightened animal by the head and held it till the
party got safely out. There is a neat Baptist Chapel at
Adbeg, Rothesay, ever pleasant and ever popular with
visitors. The Baptist Chapel here is usually crowded
in summer. Mr. Crabbe, one of Mr. Spurgeon's former

students, officiates in the said chapel. With much acceptance Mr. Spurgeon worshipped there in the morning. The chapel was crowded, many failing to get admittance.

" Mr. Spurgeon preached in front of the Rothesay Academy in the evening. He stood upon the top of the porch of the mansion of Provost Orkney, and there preached to the assembled thousands, attracted by the fame of the preacher, from Luke xiii. 10-17. There were present at least fifteen thousand. Behind us, in front of the Academy, there was a great crowd of most attentive listeners. Before us, onwards to the preacher, there was a dense mass of interested hearers. Towards our right hand, the side of the hill, on the summit of which towers the Rothesay Museum, was lined with hundreds on hundreds of hearers. The vast audience being thus seated on a natural amphitheatre, the preacher had full command of his hearers. These had come from all parts of Bute, from Largs, Millpont, and Dunoon, not a few having crossed the firth in yachts and small boats. The weather was delightful. The congregation began to assemble between three and four o'clock p.m., and before six every available seat on the sward was occupied, whilst those who arrived later had to content themselves with standing in the road leading up to the Academy.

" Mr. Spurgeon said : ' Oh that my blessed Master would look around this throng this night and find out those who are bowed down in spirit and almost in despair ! He or she who thought himself or herself most likely to be passed by, and so obscure and undeserving of Christ's regard, was most likely to obtain the blessing. Some Christians,' said the preacher, ' seem to think that it is a sin to be joyful. They are always crying out : Oh, this is a waste and howling wilderness ! Then, they

ought not to howl, but ought to rejoice. Timothy
Rogers, who was twenty-six years a prey to melancholy,
came, after all, out into the full clear light of Gospel
grace. The preacher recollected a young woman who,
he believed, was an excellent Christian, who yet thought
and said, "I am an awful hypocrite, and I do not love
the Saviour at all!" "Will you put your name to that?"
said Mr. Spurgeon. The horror upon her face was
delightful to see, and she exclaimed, "I will be torn in
pieces first." Some ministers,' he said, 'preached in
such a way that people were made gloomy and very sad
at heart. He wished hearers to follow the practice of
the man who got bad milk. "I don't care, now," said
the man, "whether there is bad milk or not, because
I keep a cow of my own." Thus, when people found
that the teaching of the pulpit did not give them comfort, they should take to the reading of their Bibles more
than they had ever done before. In that way they could
keep a cow of their own, and they would not need to
care whether the milk was good or bad. There are
some Christians,' he said, ' who always remind us of a
person who walks into the class when his face is dirty,
instead of washing it with water.' Referring to the
Liberator at His work, the preacher said, 'The way of
salvation consists of two steps—the first is out of ourselves, and the second is into Christ. None but Jesus—
that is the Gospel. Christ,' he said, 'performed this
miracle on the poor, bowed-down woman out of common
humanity; another motive was that of special property,
and a third was a peculiar antagonism to the devil.'
Mr. Spurgeon, as is usual with him, preached with great
power, and exhibited the glorious Gospel of the blessed
Lord with remarkable earnestness and clearness."

The reference to the accident in the above

needs supplementing, the fact being that Mr.
Spurgeon, Mr. Duncan, and those who were in
the carriage had the narrowest possible escape
from a violent death. Their deliverance was
entirely providential. It appears, from what I
learned of the affair, that it is a custom in
the north, with certain drivers, to allow their
horses to rush down long steep hills at a head-
long pace. While driving Mr. Duncan and his
guests, as stated above, the coachman on coming
to a declivity allowed the horses to proceed in
the customary merry fashion ; but not approving
of that mode of travelling, Mr. Spurgeon, on their
safe arrival at the foot of the hill, expressed a
desire that a more English-like manner of driving
might be practised. " Oh," said the man, " We
always go like that here." He knew more about
driving than all the preachers in the world, and
was determined to act in accordance with his
knowledge. Soon they came to another hill, and
to the discomfiture of the travellers, they at once
found themselves descending at express speed.
Then the harness broke, the man lost all control
over the horses, which presented the appearance
of frightened runaways. There was a prospect
of being knocked to pieces, and Mr. Spurgeon
confessed that his thoughts were directed to that
subject ; and the people at the roadside looked

with terror on the spectacle. At the bottom was
a zigzag road, protected by a slight fence, and
beyond this a precipice ; but the party were
delivered when the horses, instead of going straight
forward to destruction, as nineteen horses out of
twenty would have done, turned into another
road, which was an incline. Unable to keep on
at that rate up the hill, they moderated their
speed ; and when danger had passed the friend
may have come to the rescue, but not before.
He said that he never travelled so rapidly in his
life, except in an express train.

On the 5th of August, the first Monday evening prayer-meeting, after his return from the
north, a crowded congregation assembled at the
Tabernacle, doubtless expecting to hear something about their Pastor's adventures in the North.
He said he had been lately in many lone places
in Scotland, far removed from the haunts of men.
He had gone there to seek a restoration of health.
He had obtained, in a measure, what he sought,
but, owing to the numbers of persons who visited
him out of a kindly feeling, even in these remote
parts, he had scarcely known what solitude was,
and had consequently not derived that amount
of benefit, in a bodily sense, which he otherwise
would have done. He had been on many fishing
excursions, and from them had learned many

10

lessons. In that College—the one attached to the Tabernacle—they were all fishermen, but he could wish that many of the fishermen there had a little more catching bait about them than they seemed to possess. They must get the fish about them by some means or another before they were caught, and to that end a harmless pleasantry was a capital bait. Sometimes he had been blamed for giving vent to witticisms, but in his own mind he had done well by so doing, because people came to hear him, and when they did so many were caught. The fact was, it was a good catching bait. Mr. Spurgeon then proceeded to say that if persons went to fish either for fish or for human souls, they must not be fools, for if they were they would be like him when, a few days ago near Rothesay, he threw his lines into the water, and instead of watching them, turned away and allowed the fish to take off the bait without so much as being pricked by the hook. The Sunday-school was a grand place to use catching bait, but they must not allow the young fry to suck off the bait unless they bolted the hook of the Gospel. If the teachers of religion never got a bite, they should not go to sleep, but should bait their hooks afresh, and try different waters. They then might get some to bolt the bait, hook and all, just in the same way as the cod did.

Those were the sort of fellows he liked—the nibblers were scarcely any good. In conclusion he gave a description of the scenery of Scotland, and expressed his thanks for the hospitality he had received.

One or two amusing things happened in connection with his visit to Scotland this year. A correspondent thus referred to these northern services :—

" Mr. Spurgeon preached at Pollokshaws, near Glasgow, on the 1st of August. Long before the hour fixed for the beginning of the service the place of worship was besieged by crowds of people anxious to get admission, and as it was altogether impracticable to allow others than ticket-holders to pass into the place of meeting, thousands who would willingly have paid to get inside were turned away disappointed. An amusing incident is reported as having occurred at the gates, where a policeman or two and several stalwart office-bearers acted in the capacity of sentries and collected the passports. Mr. Spurgeon, having elbowed his way through the crowd as far as the gate, was asked to show and deliver his ticket ; but not being a ticket-holder the great preacher was peremptorily told to " cut his stick." Happily some persons who recognised the familiar face, greatly amused at the comical situation, nudged the policeman's elbow, and he immediately gave way. The crowds who had gone in the hope of getting admission without tickets and were excluded were addressed in the Greenbank Public Park by Mr. Spurgeon, jun. Though Mr. Spurgeon's fame as a preacher went before him like the light and radiancy of the bearded comet, his preaching at Rothesay, and we have no doubt at Pollokshaws, has exceeded expectation."

Another incident in connection with this excursion may be mentioned. Such was the pressure of the crowd that the beadle was lost sight of at the time for commencing service, and there was no one to show Mr. Spurgeon to the pulpit in accordance with the Scotch polite usage. A member of Session, however, mounted the pulpit steps, and called out in a stentorian voice that the beadle was "wanted immediately." This incident created some merriment among even a people not remarkable for their witty propensities.

At a field-meeting with his students at Clapham, both before and after dinner, Mr. Spurgeon himself told some further incidents of this journey. Among other things he was privileged to hear a sermon in Gaelic, and rather wearying of listening to what he could not understand, he whispered something to a Highland gentleman, who replied, " If ye pull his coat tail he'll soon have done."

By some means the sermon came to an end somewhat sooner than the preacher intended ; and it then transpired that he had got with the prodigal son into the far country without having had time to get him back again. Mr. Spurgeon particularly noticed the repetition of one word which sounded like *agath*, but on mentioning this he was told that it signified *and*.

After his escape from accident he was especially glad to return to the yacht. After all, he thought the sea the only really safe place. For example, you ran no risk there of being killed by a pantile.

On one of the days while he was in Scotland he dined with a leading family—a gentleman, I believe, who held a distinguished position in connection with the city of Glasgow. At dinner the Pastor, assuming a very grave face, asked this friend, " Mr. ——, are you aware that your office entitles you to go without charge through any toll-gate in England ? " Mr. —— smiled, and though not previously aware of the privilege attached to his office, quite appreciated the honour. Was it really so indeed ? When his curiosity was a little further stimulated Mr. Spurgeon, to prevent any misapprehension, added, " Yes, you are entitled to walk through, but if you take a horse you must pay."

In the field, at the students' meeting, also, he told

this anecdote of Scotland:—When I was in Arran,
quite recently, I heard of a minister who preached
in a certain church, and at the close of the service
was strongly urged to promise for a future supply,
the collection after his sermon having been unusually large. " Dear me!" said the minister, with
becoming pride, " what might your ordinary collection amount to?"   " Last Sunday it was two-
pence halfpenny."   " What is it to-day, then ? "
asked the other, expecting to hear a large sum.
" Eightpence halfpenny," was the reply.   " Woe
is me!" said the other, " for I gave sixpence of it
myself."

UNDER THE LAW OF WORKS.

I was once riding on an omnibus between
London and Edmonton, when a very self-righteous
methodist began to lament the laxity of the
English people in regard to their non-observance
of the Sabbath.   At last he referred to the conduct of Mr. Spurgeon as especially reprehensible,
for Mr. Spurgeon rode to chapel in a brougham.

" Why don't he keep the Sabbath ? *I* do," said
the man sternly, almost fiercely, and in that self-
satisfied tone common to his class.   I forget what
answer I made ; but this objection to the Pastor's
riding to chapel was not new.   Some busy
Pharisee once had the temerity to write to

Clapham on this very question, and received in reply a notification that the horse which ran in the Sunday carriage was in reality so far a Jew that he kept his Sabbath on Saturday. To make sure of this being true, I mentioned the circumstance to Mr. Spurgeon, when I found it was all right; his horse lived under the law of works and not of grace, and hence was not allowed to work on the seventh day. He usually kept two horses, and the fodder for these animals was supplied gratis by Deacon Murrell, "the gate-keeper." at the Tabernacle. "How many horses may I keep, Murrell?"—*i.e.,* "how many will *you* keep for me?"—once asked the Pastor. "Twenty," said the good-natured deacon, and meant what he said.

TABERNACLE DEACONS.

The above will remind some of the readers of this book that Mr. Spurgeon has from the first been peculiarly favoured in his deacons. They have assuredly been a kind-hearted set of men, forward in advancing Christian work, and many of them have been specially adapted for some kind of special service. Those who remember the familiar form of "Father" Olney in the past, will know that he left behind him many fragrant memories; and he was favoured by having sons who followed in his footsteps, while his grandson, the founder of the Haddon Hall Mission, is one of the benefactors of Bermondsey. In regard to serving tables, was there ever one who excelled in that department more than Mr. W. Murrell, who yearly, during Conference week, superintends the daily feeding of hundreds of ministers, besides having to provide the grand supper, at which from six to eight hundred subscribers to the College Funds sit down?

Deacon Murrell volunteered to see after the gates at the Tabernacle, and some other duties associated with that unenviable office. In all weathers his not by any means slender form might be seen, his coat closely buttoned, and his hands hidden deep down in the recesses of his side pockets. It was difficult to prevent some of the ordinary servants from accepting bribes, but woe to the deluded applicant who, in mistake, offered a gratuity to this counterpart of Bunyan's Mr. Greatheart! Once he was severely provoked by an obstinate man who refused to come out of a seat of which he had taken wrongful possession. At last, being unable to control his temper any longer, Mr. Murrell cried out to the offender, "If you go there I'll EAT you!" putting such a terrible emphasis on the threat that the man looked up, startled if not seriously alarmed.

After the service the gentleman complained to the Pastor that a very big man had threatened to eat him in the gallery. " What now, Murrell—have you been threatening to eat a man ? " was subsequently asked of his friend and horse-keeper by Mr. Spurgeon. " Well," replied the deacon, " I did say so ; he would not get out of the seat, and I did not know what else to say."

A Summer Festival.

Formerly it was Mr. Spurgeon's custom to hold some outdoor services on the farm of Mr. Abraham, at Minster Lovell, in Oxfordshire. In reference to one of these festivals *The Baptist* remarked :—

" The interest which his visits have awakened is not confined to the immediate locality, for his audience is drawn from the country round within a radius of five-and-twenty miles. The narrow lanes which converge to the centre of attraction can only be compared to the roads which lie between London and Epsom on a Derby Day. The bicycle and the barouche, the perambulator and the postchaise, the two-wheeled tumbril and the four-horse coach, indicate the extremes between which the graduated contrivances for locomotion are pressed into the service of bearing their living freights. Hundreds had to avail themselves of the marrow-bone stage. Some who left home in the early morning to be in time scarcely succeeded in completing the return journey on the same day. That such enthusiasm was manifested to hear the Gospel is an evidence that the clergy have not a spiritual monopoly in perhaps the most ritualistic county in the kingdom.

" The services are held under a clump of trees near the spot where the Ringwood Oak stood for many years as a grand relic of the once famous Wychwood Forest. Very little of the forest now remains, most of the land being under cultivation. Mr. Abraham, who farms some 600 acres, makes a capital host, and to him is due the successful arrangements which make the annual visit of Mr. Spurgeon so pleasant to all concerned. His daughters vie with one another in attending upon the guests, who dine in relays at the well-furnished table of the house, while his sons are very busy in making arrangements for stabling the horses. Little groups were to be seen under the grateful shade of the oaks at luncheon, preparatory to the first service, which was held at half-past two o'clock. The scene is one of the most picturesque conceivable. From the house may be seen, in the valley of the Windrush, the ruins of the castellated mansion of the Lovells, made famous by the tragic incident in the song of ' The Mistletoe Bough.' On the slope of the nearest hill rising above the river is the scattered village founded by Feargus O'Connor for a working man's settlement, every house having its garden capable of yielding sufficient to maintain a moderate family in comfort. In the distance the Chilterns form the sky-line, the White Horse at Wantage and the Farringdon Clump being conspicuous objects.

" When Mr. Spurgeon ascended the waggon to commence the afternoon service, there must have been at least 1,500 people present. The singing was hearty if not highly artistic, and during the prayer the Wesleyan brethren betrayed their presence by the responses which they could not restrain. The preacher was at

his best, and the subject chosen, ' I will be as the dew
unto Israel,' furnished abundant scope for illustration
by metaphors which appealed to the bucolic mind. Tea
was provided in a large marquee, and, as the various
parties were refreshed, they wandered in companies
over the pleasure-grounds which surround the house.
It required a very slight effort of the imagination to
picture the Feast of Tabernacles, when the faithful
assembled to tell of the goodness and mercy of God,
and to sing praises unto the Most High. Such an
opportunity for Christian intercourse is of incalculable
value to those Christians who, in out-of-the-way places,
receive but slight help in their combat with sin and
labour for the Lord, and many must have returned
nerved to fresh resolution, or aroused by a new
enthusiasm to witness for Christ in their own sphere
of life and service !

"As the time for evening service drew on, Mr. Charlesworth and several of the ministers present extemporised
a meeting, the speakers being allowed five minutes each.
The crowd, swollen now to upwards of 2,000, settled
down to the principal service of the day. The evening
was calm, and the westering sun threw around the
scene a weird charm, as the lengthening shadows of
the trees contrasted with the strangely-blended hues
which make a July sunset so beautiful. The air seemed
to hold a solemn stillness, and there was nothing to
break the spell. We never witnessed an open-air
service before when everything so conspired to favour
the preacher. At times the deep hush of the rapt
audience was literally awe-inspiring. It is no exaggera-
tion to say that a wave of spiritual emotion broke over
the assembly, few hearts, if any, being insensible to its
influence. From the first sentence in the prayer which
commenced the service to the last words of the bene-

diction with which it closed, the preacher had the audience in his grip. Never did he enforce his ministry of reconciliation with more earnest appeals, nor move an audience by more tender pleadings. As the assembly broke up we heard more than one minister exclaim, ' We shall hear of this service again.' "

SOME SPECIAL OCCASIONS

"*Still, a minister, wherever he is, is a minister, and should recollect that he is on duty.* A policeman or a soldier may be off duty, but a minister never is. Even in our recreations we should still pursue the great object of our lives ; for we are called to be diligent in season and out of season. There is no position in which we may be placed but the Lord may come with the question, 'What doest thou here, Elijah ? ' and we ought to be able at once to answer, 'I have something to do for Thee even here, and I am trying to do it.' The bow, of course, must be at times unstrung or else it will lose its elasticity ; but there is no need to cut the string. . . . A minister should be like a certain chamber which I saw at Beaulieu, in the New Forest, in which a cobweb is never seen. It is a large lumber-room, and is never swept ; yet no spider ever defiles it with the emblems of neglect. It is roofed with chestnut, and for some reason, I know not what, spiders will not come near that wood by the year together. The same thing was mentioned to me in the corridors of Winchester school : I was told, 'No spiders ever come here.' Our minds should be equally clear of idle habits."—*Lectures to my Students,* i. 181-2.

VI.

SOME SPECIAL OCCASIONS.

A VIEW FROM THE DEACONS' SEATS.

THERE are several ways of passing into the Metropolitan Tabernacle ; and these are tolerably familiar to country visitors, as well as to knowing Londoners. It is also generally acknowledged that London crowds are dangerous, unless carefully managed by suitable regulations. If a crowd be regularly attracted to one building, and each individual be visibly anxious to secure a good place, not hesitating to use hands and elbows in working towards the front, the specified regulations must include locked gates, as well as carefully-guarded side-entrances, which are only available for ticket-holders. The regular attendant at the Metropolitan Tabernacle has necessarily to have his seat reserved, otherwise he would find himself an unequal competitor with the casual hearer, especially if the said casual hearer happened to be an early riser on Sunday morning. Thus there are three ways of going to hear Mr. Spurgeon. We may be one of the favoured few—few, comparatively, when the irregular hearers number so large a proportion of the weekly congregation—who, as seat-holders, walk directly into the building, while the impatient crowd of the court is kept at bay by doors securely bolted and barred. Secondly, should we not rank among pew-holders, and still feel painfully conscious of not possessing strength, either of muscle or of nerve, to hold our own in the column besieging the entrance, we take care to provide ourselves with an early admission ticket, entitling us to the right of waiting in one of the aisles before the doors are opened. In this position a visitor may very profitably exercise the virtue of patience while occupying a standpoint whence he watches the thousands who comfortably sit at ease in the pews, and calculates as to the chances of securing a seat. Should we, however, belong to neither of the classes described, our ingress into the great building will, perforce, become a more interesting, though, possibly, a less pleasant process. We shall take up our position under the portico "early;" we shall learn that minutes may be long or short according to the circumstances of the situation.

Then comes relief in a sudden, exciting manner.

Bolts shoot backward, and the apparently electrified crowd, as if in response to a preconcerted signal, move forward *en masse ;* for, once inside the chapel, all regulations are summed up in one —First come first served.

On a certain Sabbath morning I dispensed with each of the methods above specified of entering that institution of modern London, the Metropolitan Tabernacle. By special favour I occupied a seat on the platform behind the preacher. These seats are twelve in number, forming a double row. They are padded, are lined with crimson velvet, and have arms somewhat after the manner of a first-class railway carriage. Without question they are luxurious in all their appointments ; but then they are for the deacons. A deaconship at the Tabernacle is no sinecure, and the occupiers of these seats are known to be worthy of the accommodation they receive.

Suppose it is half-past ten a.m., or thereabouts when I am politely ushered into my "deacon's seat," and commence to study the extraordinary scene. It is spring-time—the sun is high in the heavens ; but within the building the gas is burning, while the view is partially interrupted by a misty atmosphere in sympathy with the slight fog without doors. The immense area, which, to a stranger, might appear to be already nearly

11

filled, must undergo the process of filling till it is packed. The movements of the people can only be compared with the motion of a swarm of insects, not, however, eager and impatient like the crowd outside; for the new arrivals are merely taking up their regularly-appointed places.

Onward move the great hands of the giant clock overhead, until they point to 10.40, when we witness a transformation scene both lively and extensive. Hitherto the "regulars" and "irregulars" had leisurely entered by side-doors, with the comfortable consciousness of being privileged persons; but now all the main front entrances are opened at once, and in pour the broad living streams, to occupy, to the last inch, the standing-room of what appears to be an already overcrowded building. Look this way or that way, or take a general view, and it will be hard to distinguish between aisles and pews. The new comers are manifestly a little excited in their anxiety to find seats; and yet the bustle is not altogether like any other bustle which is witnessed in public buildings. The coughing, talking, and feet-shuffling produce a compound sound peculiar to the Tabernacle; and this is instantly hushed when Mr. Spurgeon appears on the platform.

When the first word of the service is uttered,

the multitude of faces are all turned in one direction—towards the preacher. Those who occupy seats in proximity to Mr. Spurgeon's table may perhaps have observed that the tones of his voice seem to be nicely adapted to the requirements of those who are near, as well as to those who are farther away. To persons sitting near they are never unpleasantly loud; to those in the remotest corner they are loud enough, while they are never indistinct. Not that so vast a concourse can be addressed, even by a man of the greatest lung-power, without a strong effort, though in this instance the strain is barely observed even by those who listen immediately beneath the clock. As seen from the deacon's standpoint, it is also interesting to note how the leviathan congregation allows itself to be managed. It is subject to certain influences as if it were one great being instead of six thousand atoms. It has its recognised coughing times; by way of acknowledging a touch of humour, it smiles like one vast creature which is particularly sensitive. Then it sings "faster" or "slower," according to directions, and is in all respects most admirably managed.

While reading the concluding verse of "Rock of Ages" the Pastor is visibly affected, just as, a few minutes before, he seemed to catch and diffuse the spirit of "that wonderful Gospel chapter," Isaiah lv. Anon, the quiet earnestness of the sermon seems to extend its influence throughout the entire space of the building, until the rapt attention of the crowd, as they listen to exposition and appeal based on the words, " *Without money and without price,*" is found to kindle feelings akin to actual awe. To handle what are called commonplace or hackneyed texts in a manner strikingly original is the *forte* of a great man ; the ability to do this with consummate art is characteristic of the genius of Mr. Spurgeon.

It is very common for preachers who stand up before large assemblies to fix their eye on a particular individual ; a spectator who views the scene from the deacons' seats at the Metropolitan Tabernacle is extremely liable to find himself doing the same odd kind of thing. There are "characters" enough in the spacious area, if one can only single them out and read their faces. There sits a man in one of the middle aisles of the area ; he is middle-aged, full-faced, and altogether in his *tout ensemble* resembles one who makes some pretension to self-culture. Though he uses no pencil and note-book, his brains are, probably, busily at work taking down what he sees. Let us suppose him to be the representative of some slumberless daily newspaper, which will be sure to place the public in possession of ample information should anything special in the morning's proceedings attract his attention. Single out another, and perhaps you will not be far wide of the mark if you set him down to be a 'cute Yankee editor on the look-out for something piquant about the Britishers wherewith to regale his readers in some obscure corner of the American continent. Do you think it possible you may be mistaken? Look again, and ask yourself if the worthy fellow's features and wearing apparel, when put together, do not spell JONATHAN as completely as can ever be done by eight letters? A fair sprinkling of country pastors are sure to be present. Fix your eye on a Baptist, and he will be found in a genial humour; for when so vast an assembly gathers in a Baptist Chapel he thinks, with some show of reason, that his principles are in the ascendant. Select an Independent, and you will judge from his looks that he has not much to complain about; for, after all, this same preacher has wonderfully stimulated the cause of Nonconformity. Besides these, members of the Establishment, of various grades, must be on a level with the rest of the world, and to accomplish this and complete their education they must needs go to "hear Spurgeon." If the Anglican be an Evangelical, he will be abundantly edified ; he will go away regretting that the Pastor is not Archbishop of Canterbury. Should he side with the Ritualists, he will look pitiful and ill at ease —he may even sit with the scowl of contempt playing about his eyes. Should he be of the Broad school, he will be sufficiently charitable to take things as they come. As I view the spacious area from my velvet-lined deacon's pew, I know that the Tabernacle is a common meeting-ground for all the characters mentioned, as well as for many others who might be included in the category.

But it is now time to confess that when we sit in the deacons' seats we occupy a comfortable pew, but, while doing so, sacrifice much that would be cheaply purchased by a hard bench with a deal back. When heard from behind, Mr. Spurgeon is heard to disadvantage. He is not a preacher who should be listened to with a pillar interrupting the view, nor with closed eyes. His features speak as well as his tongue, and this part of the sermon was almost entirely missed while I kept company with the deacons on the platform. As viewed from the ordinary pews, these portly church officers appear to be so luxuriously accommodated, and to be in themselves such models of decorum, that dozens of times have they been envied both on account of their state and their station. Let the truth henceforth be known—that, like men of self-denial, they are content to forego much for the sake of their office.

A word may be added relative to the Weekly Offering collection. The boxes used at the morning service were brought into one of the vestries after the crowd had dispersed. How high a figure the total reached nobody knew, for, as Sunday is a day of rest, the money would not be counted until the following morning. Gold, silver, and copper pieces, together with little packets neatly tied with thread, made up the motley heap. One miniature parcel enclosed fifteen shillings from " A Working Man." When the whole mass was placed in a strong black bag, I ventured to raise it for the sake of testing its weight.

" It's pretty heavy," remarked an affable deacon, who appeared to be the Chancellor of the Exchequer of the establishment.

I anticipated that the parcel would not be found to be a bag of feathers. It was certainly the " heaviest " collection I had ever set eyes upon, for it was as much as one could conveniently raise from the table with one arm.

AT A WHITSUNTIDE FESTIVAL.

" Are you going with Mr. Spurgeon, sir ? " politely asked an active carriage attendant on the departure platform of the Great Eastern Railway terminus in London a few minutes before the starting of the midday Cambridge express-train. The man was evidently a shrewd reader of character, or he would not so happily have hit on the truth at first guess, or have drawn so correct an inference from my mien, appearance, and tourist-bag. I gave the honest fellow an answer in the affirmative, secured a comfortable corner-seat, and in a few minutes the train was travelling at a rapid speed through Tottenham marshes, our destination being Willingham, in Cambridgeshire.

On our arrival at Cambridge soon after one, it is clearly manifest that Mr. Spurgeon is expected, and a railway official acquaints us with the fact that large numbers of persons have gone forward by the early trains. After a brief delay we are again in motion, and this time we are on the Wisbeach branch, and at each small station even the porters are on the *qui vive*. At any rate, one of these worthies, who had probably heard a false rumour that the preacher of the day was not coming, shouted in a kind of suppressed tone of

triumph, " There he is ! " just as our train drew
up alongside the platform. We arrive at Long
Stanton shortly after two, from whence we drive to
Willingham through a rich flat country, the air
having been made delightfully cool by the storms
of the day before. Throughout the route numbers
of country people, dressed in holiday attire, scru-
tinise the carriage which carries the Pastor with
keen curiosity ; while in the village proper a
considerable crowd has assembled. Of course
business in general is suspended ; banners enliven
the street ; householders appear to be keeping
open house, though provision for a thousand, more
or less, is served in a farmyard and barn hard by.
In a word, the village is *en fête*, and that un-
answerable authority, " the oldest inhabitant " of
Willingham, is well aware that the doings now
in progress surpass everything which has come
within the range of his experience.

Willingham is situated in the midst of a purely
agricultural district, and is some two miles away
from the Long Stanton station. The living is
a good one ; the parish covers an area of five
thousand acres ; and in Puritan times, under
its godly rector, Mr. Bradshaw, the village was
remarkable for its piety. In those days, there
were " fourscore-and-ten praying families " resident in the parish ; and a portion of these, with

Mr. Bradshaw, the ejected rector, appear to have been the founders of the Nonconformist interest which has flourished in Willingham from that time to this.   The place has its pleasant memories, and the Willingham of to-day presents us with some of the most favourable aspects of English village life.   It acknowledges no great land-owner for its sole lord.   Small proprietorships are the rule, and the lords of these, comfortably housed in their villa or cottage freeholds, look as though they knew how to enjoy the privileges of freedom.   If an Englishman's house is his castle, there are many lords and castles at Willingham.   The gardens in the rear of the houses are not the least extraordinary feature of the village, and they completely verify all I have heard in praise of Cambridgeshire horticulture. The gardens are commonly found to be of great length, and they are usually planted with favourite fruit-bearing trees.   I was given to understand that in ground attached to the houses of this small place there are not less than fifty acres of gooseberry-bushes in a luxuriant state of cul-tivation.

The advertisements announced that Mr. Spurgeon would preach the first of his two sermons at three o'clock ; and, as that hour drew near, the people who had hitherto thronged the village street

adjourned to an adjacent meadow, there to com-
pose a compact multitude. A spacious marquee
had been erected ; but, ample as its area may
have appeared to the contractors, it was ludicrously
small when measured against the space required ;
and hence to speak from a waggon on the green-
sward seemed to be the only possible arrangement
that could be reasonably made. Having, with
considerable difficulty, threaded his way through
the throng, the preacher ascended the "pulpit," and
found himself in the centre of a sea of upturned
faces ; and, confessing an inability to speak from
the back of his head, he notifies in which direction
he will chiefly look. The text is taken from
I Cor. xv. 10 : "By the grace of God I am what
I am ; " and the sermon, with its fervent deli-
neations and soul-stirring appeals, was admirably
adapted to produce a lasting effect on the mixed
multitude of hearers. The purport of the sermon
was—everybody had some ailment ; but Christ
was " the mighty doctor of grace."

At the conclusion of this service, the people
returned to the village to drink tea, which was not
difficult to obtain, as everybody still appeared to
be keeping open house, and provision for a hungry
multitude was made at the farmstead before
mentioned. Mr. Spurgeon and a select number
of friends drank tea together in one of the long,

secluded gardens for which Willingham is or should be renowned.

At the evening service the sermon was preceded by a characteristic address from Mr. William Olney, one of the most active of the deacons at the Tabernacle. When Mr. Spurgeon again stood forward, he was greeted as before by the upturned faces of persons who still drank in his words with unabated eagerness. The text was taken from the dying words of King David to his son Solomon, " If thou seek Him, He shall be found of thee." All that David said was good ; but the last words of such a father to such a son as Solomon were especially solemn.

I. They represented our greatest want—they needed their God.

II. David told Solomon how his great need might be supplied—" If thou seek Him."

Lastly, the text had a finger—*Thou.* The preacher went on to show that while the young had a text all to themselves, the old needed not to be discouraged. Some calculations had been made to show that people are seldom converted after forty-five, and as they grow older the chances that they will ever become partakers of saving grace proportionately diminished. In the opinion of Mr. Spurgeon such notions were as ridiculous as they were unscriptural, and statistics were frequently little else than a means of telling lies by figures.

The evening scene was one to be remembered. Parts of the surrounding district had only lately been visited by storms; but during the delivery of the sermon the peace of a summer evening settled over Willingham. A soft breeze carried the sweet scents of the fresh blossoming country on its bosom; birds were merrily singing in the trees and hedges; while the setting sun on one side of the horizon, and the rising moon on the other side, seemed to be looking each other in the face while they supplied the preacher with materials for illustration. The spectacle was very striking as a scene of rural peace and enjoyment. The powerful voice of Mr. Spurgeon rung out loud and clear, reaching to the utmost limit of the crowd. Individuals representative of various classes of sinners were singled out, reasoned with, and appealed to, the text in each instance being driven home to the heart and conscience—" If thou seek Him, He shall be found of thee."

Thus further proof was given, if that were needed, of the hold which Mr. Spurgeon still retains on every class. I inquired of a Cambridgeshire peasant what he thought of the sermon. " Oh ! " replied the poor fellow, " it was lovely ; I wish he had kept on all night."

With the Students.

Probably a good many people who once thought otherwise are coming round to the conclusion that "Spurgeon's students" are an institution called into existence by the requirements of the modern Church. While there will be differences of opinion in regard to the young fellows' general fitness for an arduous calling, the majority of judges will concede that they are men of enterprise, who can battle with difficulties and bear hardship. They have many traits which mark their individuality, and they strive to do credit to the common cause, and to be worthy of their schoolmasters. If you will, you may count these young men too daring, too energetic, or too assuming ; but while the field is the world, and the world remains what it is, there will be plenty of others who will think that there is room both for the workers and their singularities. It is well known that there are persons, sensitive and not too charitable, who affect to look down on the Tabernacle collegians as innovators or interlopers, or perhaps even as trespassers, who monopolise spheres which common fairness would reserve for better people. To be criticised is a privilege as well as a penalty ; for without critics public men would not know their own weaknesses. As regards the " students " in question, we should in justice remember that a very large percentage of those who settle in London make their own spheres. Another large proportion, who remove to the Colonies and to the United States, cease to be in anybody's way—so far as England is concerned.

Mr. Spurgeon never disguises the fact that the College is his best-beloved Institution. He well knows that his system may have its weak points, but that is only saying it is human. In spite of real or imaginary shortcomings, the College is nurtured as a powerful evangelistic agency. It has even been hinted that he expects, or at least hopes to see, a successor to himself come forth from the classes. Such a genius has not yet arisen ; to expect his advent may perhaps savour of enthusiasm. The president is a man of faith ; there is time enough yet.

Founded and presided over by so shrewd a judge of human nature and of human motives, this College differs from the ordinary run of theological seminaries. The aim of the tutors is very clearly defined. They do not despise learning, but still wish to turn out preachers rather than scholars, and to accomplish their purpose they cannot complain of any want of material. Every candidate is well aware that he will have to pass a searching examination, and that the aim of the examiners will be to discover his aptitude for work—the quality of the human metal—instead of being guided in their decision by what he already knows. ' The judges put down piety at a higher value than Greek and Latin ; and they believe that love for mankind is better than a mathematical brain. Come what will, the applicant, if he be a man of common sense, is thoroughly assured that he will be judged on his own merits. He needs no friend at court to advance his interests, the recommendation of his pastor being merely a certificate of character. Nothing can be more unprejudiced than this method of election. Even if it were true, which it is not, that it chiefly attracts the plebeian element, even that would be preferable to being spoken of as a pretentious Nonconformist college reserved almost exclusively for those who can help themselves.

Having survived his probation, the " student " feels that he is a unit in a society which exists to promote the conversion of mankind ; and while his interests are not separate from those of his denomination, he will throughout life retain a feeling of clannishness. It is well that it is so, for his difficulties and discouragements are of no common order. Go whither he will, he must resist the opposition of prejudice—a prejudice founded on the poor fellow's supposed lack of good breeding and early advantages. It is surprising how long and correct peoples' memories are when they have to do with things they might gracefully forget. "Spurgeon's student" is ofter found to be a suffering victim of this persecuting retentiveness. People remember—and if they do not really know they suspect—that he was originally intended for some trade, that he was actually apprenticed, and that he would even now be working at a bench had he not, through some mischance, found his way into college. They do not stop to ask themselves whether similar things might not apply to numbers of other ministers who have passed through other seminaries. Provided only that a college can boast of a certain kind of prestige, the inmates are looked upon as scholars and gentlemen, who have been directed into their proper avocation. Let us not disparage one class at the expense of another, but give both their due, because neither class can afford to throw stones at the other. In common fairness we are bound to judge of men by their works. The cultured man will find his proper sphere, and between him and the more humble, though perhaps not less useful, evangelist, there need be no rivalry. Ministerial successes should be measured by conver-

12

sions, not by the literary quality of the sermons preached ; and so that men are brought in from the bondage of sin into the liberty of Christ, it is hardly worth while to dispute about the polish of the instruments. Who, on looking at an elegant cabinet, asks if the artificer had five fingers on each hand, if he was legally apprenticed, and if the tools used were those of approved makers ? The carving is there, and we give the workman his due. If we look at their work from all sides in this spirit, we shall find that " Spurgeon's students " have more than earned their salt. They have established a large number of new churches ; they have reclaimed thousands of people who might never have been hauled in from ruin by the kid-gloved hands of a more " regular " agency. They are trained to endure hardship and toil. In a sense, they are undoubtedly innovators ; at times, perhaps, they are somewhat too bold and outspoken ; but still some of them have become sufficiently distinguished to rank among the chief apostles of Bristol, Rawdon, or even Regent's Park—those classic retreats for well-to-do aspirants and gentlemen's sons.

The ordinary " Spurgeon's student " has many characteristics which bespeak his training and ruling taste. Perhaps he would be a gainer were he to rub off some of his idiosyncrasies ; but such

as cling naturally to him are best left alone.
With rare exceptions, he never affects the fine
gentleman ; he does not proclaim his profession
through the tailor ; with his black tie and felt hat
he apparently cultivates a *nonchalance* in dress not
readily understood in a fashionable age, when
ecclesiastical exquisites need not despair of
shining as centre attractions in West End drawing-rooms. Thus it happens that the " student's "
friends say he has no sham about him ; that he
wishes to pass simply for what he is—an evangelist ; or if settled, a plain pastor. His severer
critics say he is an enthusiast, an imitator of the
manners and tones of one man, and that his
sermons are declamation. In summing up the
evidence of these opposite witnesses, remember
that man naturally imitates ; that it is well-nigh
impossible for classes to come into daily contact
with one master mind and not contract a few of
his mannerisms. To the young men concerned
I would say, Strive against a natural propensity
which will provoke ridicule and loss of power.
To be peculiar is not necessarily to be weak,
though if he try to be peculiar it is a sure sign
that the man is naturally a weak man.

What has the College done ? According to
the last returns, 722 have been educated, and
there are 547 of these who still labour as pastors,

missionaries, or evangelists. There are twenty-one without pastorates ; forty-seven pastors and seven students have died ; nine are permanently invalided ; while seventy-five names have been removed from the roll, not in all cases "from causes which imply any dishonour," as many are working in other denominations. There are 66,835 members attached to the Churches of the Pastors' College Association.

CHRISTMAS DAY AT THE ORPHANAGE.

The Christmas morning to which particular allusion is now made was hailed by the inmates of the Stockwell Orphanage with all the enthusiasm that had characterised former years ; how, indeed, could it be otherwise, when the day dawned with promises of feasting and merry-making quite after the heart of Young England, who has found a home in that well-known Institution ? While the weather was cold, foggy, and muddy, the aspect of the dining-room presented a cheerful contrast to the reigning gloom without. The ample area was decorated with flags, evergreens, and mottoes, until it partially resembled a baronial hall of olden times, and numbers of visitors were found passing a holiday hour in inspecting the preparations. Callers and stragglers, who dine late, and who are desirous of seeing all they can before dinner, may find a sight worth looking at on Christmas Day at Stockwell—something to educate the heart as well as feed the mind ; and should they leave a donation behind them, the remembrance of what they have done will make music in their souls when they themselves sit down to the feast. So, at any rate, would good George Herbert have said, and George Herbert was right.

Soon after noon a carriage is heard rattling into the grounds, and this, together with the cheers of the boys, is an intimation that Mr. and Mrs. Spurgeon have arrived. Before dinner is laid on the tables a Board-meeting may have to be held ; and while more serious business is in progress, fresh loungers are coming in to show their interest in the arrangements. The kitchen appears to possess extraordinary attractions, and well may this be so ; for vast as is the quantity of food to be prepared, the admirable apparatus at the command of the cooks sits easily beneath its burden, and even seems to make light of it.

After some further unavoidable delay, the boys and girls are marshalled, shortly before two, to be marched into their places, when dinner is served. Substantial joints of roast beef follow

one another from the kitchen, each fresh arrival
being handed over to an amateur carver at a
side-table. In the meantime, Mr. Spurgeon re-
minds the boys of the gratitude they owe to God
for sending them friends who, in their kindness
of heart, have provided so rich an abundance of
good fare. The youngsters quite appreciate their
President's remarks, and show that they understand their obligations by the hearty cheers which
shake the building, a fair proportion of the noise
being made in honour of the gentlemen who
presented the boxes of plums and the new
shillings. Other cheers follow, for standing in
the room are certain tried friends of the Institution who merit the boys' affection, and this is
especially true of the President, who is hailed
with deafening acclamations as the orphans' best
earthly friend. At length the noise is succeeded
by a calm ; grace is sung. "And now, my
boys," says Mr. Spurgeon, "I hope you will
heartily enjoy yourselves." The beef, which is
the best that the London market can supply, is
speedily disposed of ; and next comes a proces-
sion of plum-puddings borne by a regiment of
"old boys," who are now out in the world making
headway on their own account. After the
puddings have shared the fate of the beef, there
succeeds a still greater pleasure—each orphan is

allowed to retire, and to carry with him to the playground his box of plums, the sweet orange, and the new shilling.

When well enough to do so, and when in England, it has been Mr. Spurgeon's custom to dine with the working staff of the Orphanage on Christmas Day. The last time that he did so was in 1885, when he was accompanied by Mrs. Spurgeon ; and he had then not been since 1881. In the last report of the Institution Mr. Spurgeon thus refers to the work in progress :—

"Let those who have aided us in any manner only look in upon the Institution at Stockwell, and the sight will well repay them. What a beautiful square of buildings! What a noble open space in the centre! Then see the boys and girls. Nobody ever said that they looked miserable : it would be too transparent a falsehood. Did you ever see more happy faces in all the world ? These bear no brand of pauperdom, and wear no trace of being crushed down by hard workhouse discipline. Many a father has felt that if he were suddenly taken away he could desire no better shelter for his children. One minister expressed that sentiment at one of our meetings, and within two years he had fallen asleep, and two of his boys were with us. These dear

children, often the descendants of sickly fathers,
are, as a rule, in splendid condition ; in fact, the
average of health is far above that which is
common in the best families. While they are
with us they receive a good solid education, and
are surrounded with gracious influences ; and
when they go from us, as a rule, they succeed in
life, and become useful and honourable members
of society. We have received the highest testimony from practical men as to the result produced by the Stockwell Orphanage training.
Thus, instead of pining in poverty, and either
dying of want or growing up in ignorance, the
children are carefully housed and prayerfully
trained, and rise into manhood to be an honour
to their homes and a benefit to society. Meanwhile, their widowed mothers have been succoured,
delivered from hopeless want, and encouraged
to bring up the rest of their charge. Friends, we
are partners in a very blessed enterprise. Our
Lord approves of it, His people delight in it,
and even men of the world have nothing to say
against it. This work for orphans is one of the
best aids to the Gospel : it stops the mouth of
adversaries. It is fit that the preacher of free
grace should be able to point to his five hundred
fatherless ones, and say, ' See the fruit of the
doctrines of grace.' Those who are saved by

faith alone are yet zealous to maintain good works. To them also, ' pure religion and undefiled before God and the Father is this, to visit the fatherless and the widows in their affliction, and to keep himself unspotted from the world.'

" Our experience confirms us in the practice of THE SEPARATE HOME SYSTEM. We have not huge wards, nor vast barracks, but houses and families after the fashion of ordinary society. The loss of home and parental influence is a calamity to a child, and the wisest course is to minimise the loss as far as possible by keeping up the family form. Covering an area of nearly four acres, in one of the healthiest suburbs of London, the Orphanage is admirably adapted for its purpose. Each home is complete in itself, and each family has its own ' mother.' The boys dine in one common hall according to families ; the girls' meals are all prepared in their respective houses ; and it is a rule that both boys and girls assist in all the domestic duties of the establishment. Family worship is conducted in each department morning and evening, and the children learn the text for the day from Mr. Spurgeon's Almanack. The terrace on the left-hand side of the quadrangle, with the schools over the centre block, is designed for two hundred and fifty boys, and the terrace on the right for an equal number of girls. The proof of the pudding is in the eating, and in countless ways the excellence of the home system shows itself to those who observe its working.

"Under our system careful supervision of each child is possible, and the best sanitary, moral, and religious conditions are secured. Though we cannot change human nature, nor make even good children perfect, we can do better for them in family groups than if we had them in great masses, and packed them away in grosses, like steel pens. Individual character comes out better in small groups than in large regiments.

"The Institution is UNSECTARIAN : the question of the denominational connection of the parents has no influence with the Committee in considering an application. No child is prejudiced as a candidate by the creed of his parents. Why should he be ? In a matter of pure philanthropy, sectarian preferences should have no weight ; although the characters of the parents and their usefulness in the Church of God constitute in some cases a plea for a more speedy reception of their little ones ; yet if Christian principles were lacking in the father the child should not be punished on that account ; on the contrary, there may be all the greater need that the little one should come under religious training.

" The supreme desire of the Committee of Management is that the children shall be instructed in the truths of our common Christianity, renewed in spirit by the Holy Ghost, and brought up in the nurture and admonition of the Lord. We are more concerned that the children should become disciples of Christ than devotees of a sect; and for this we will both pray and labour. . . .

" The Institution is OPEN TO ALL CLASSES OF THE COMMUNITY. No one section of society has the preference. In considering the claims of an orphan, the station in life occupied by the parents has small influence in the counsels of the Committee.

To secure the admission of a destitute fatherless child, NO PATRONAGE IS REQUIRED, AND NO PURCHASE OF VOTES. The most helpless and deserving are *selected* by a Committee, who give the first place to the greatest need.

" The children are NOT DRESSED IN A UNIFORM to mark them as the recipients of charity. We cannot endure this common piece of folly.

" In the arrangements of the Schools our object is to impart *a plain but thorough* ENGLISH *education*, in order to fit the boys for commercial pursuits. In addition to the ordinary subjects, they are taught elementary science, drawing, shorthand, and vocal music. As the boys attain the age for leaving, little or no difficulty is experienced in finding employers who are willing to receive them. Many of the old boys are now occupying good positions in large houses of business, three of them are pastors of churches, and two have resigned first-rate appointments to labour in connection with the Salvation Army. It is a joy to us to know that many others are engaged in works of usefulness, while a far larger number are members of the Christian Church.

"For the girls a plain solid education is attempted in the Schools, and thorough domestic training in the Homes. The Trustees will be glad to give special training where there are special capacities, and as openings occur for female talent they will be glad to have girls able to enter them. The special vocation of the girls must be left to their friends to determine on leaving : our usual plan is to ensure that, as far as possible, they shall be thoroughly fitted for domestic service in good families ; but we are anxious to be guided by the providence of God, and the opportunities which offer themselves. No doubt the better the education, if it be of a really practical kind, the better is the child's chance in life."

SUMMARY OF ADMISSIONS.

London 717
Country 358
Wales 17
Scotland 1
Ireland 2
Isle of Wight 4

Total 1,099.

PARENTAGE OF THE CHILDREN :—

Mechanics 261
Shopkeepers and Salesmen . . . 171
Manufacturers and Tradesmen . . 161
Labourers, Porters, and Carmen . . 159
Warehousemen and Clerks . . . 117
Mariners and Watermen . . . 38
Ministers and Missionaries . . . 33
Commercial Travellers 21
Farmers and Florists 21
Railway Employés 19
Cab Proprietors and Coachmen . . 18
Schoolmasters and Teachers . . . 17
Policemen and Custom House Officers . 13
Commission Agents 11
Accountants 11
Postmen and Sorters 8
Surgeons and Dentists 6
Journalists 5
Solicitors 4
Soldiers 2
Fireman 1
Architect 1
Gentleman 1

Total 1,099.

RELIGIOUS PROFESSION OF PARENTS.

Church of England	429
Baptist	264
Congregational	121
Wesleyan	101
Presbyterian	22
Roman Catholic	3
Brethren	4
Moravian	1
Bible Christian	2
Society of Friends	1
Not specified	151

Total 1,099.

The head master is the Rev. V. J. Charlesworth, and the working staff have all along, by their efficiency and sympathy, earned the often-expressed gratitude of the President.

THE COLPORTEURS.

The Colportage Association is also an evangelistic agency the influence of which extends into many of the most out-of-the-way corners of the country. When health permitted it has been usual for Mr. Spurgeon to address the men, many of whom visit London in May of each year. The agents are hard-working fellows, and besides selling books, they visit the people in their houses, and even preach the Gospel in places where otherwise the Gospel would hardly be heard.

There are now seventy-six agents employed, and
seven book agents; and in the last year these
sold pure literature to the amount of £9,525,
representing a distribution of 457,527 Bibles
and books, besides 320,504 periodicals. Mr. Spurgeon, in common with all who are acquainted
with it, are of opinion that this work should be
extended, and that Christian people should manifest more interest in the colporteurs' operations.
Certainly, its importance is second to no other
Christian work, and in proportion as the good
done is understood and appreciated, people will
extend to such a genuine Home Mission their
cordial support.

On the last occasion that he addressed the
men in May, 1885, Mr. Spurgeon remarked that
while there were old faces present that he was
glad to see again, there were also some new
hands, to all of whom he wished prosperity.
It was hoped that the first would not become
weary, and that the younger men would find
themselves in happy spheres. Though many
had found it otherwise, the past year had been
a good time for colporteurs: the sales had not
declined, and the higher success achieved had
encouraged them all. Though he was not going
to preach on the text " Sell the books," that
was the first thing a colporteur had to do. They

might be good men in other respects, but they did not excel as colporteurs if they did not push the sales. It was just the same with students in the college; they had first of all to be good preachers. Thus the main object of their calling must not be missed. Yankee book-agents had the reputation of being terrible fellows: they would never leave a house without an order, even though it might be an order to get off the premises; and one of the fraternity was said to have so much " cheek," that when struck by lightning in the face—his strongest point—the fluid glanced off to kill an animal some yards away. In a sense, this " cheek " was a good thing, although they would not do much without perseverance. They wanted men to sell books to people who thought that they did not want to buy them. They had no reason to be ashamed of their wares, which were good to sell and good to buy. It was then shown that a colporteur would be judged of in a district by his usefulness. As they loved their Master, therefore, let them abound in all good works to His glory, forasmuch as their labour was not in vain in the Lord.

The Rev. W. Corden Jones, at the Depository, Temple Street, Newington, S.E., supplies all particulars on application.

TWO THOUSAND PRINTED SERMONS.

13

"Our ministry is a testimony that no new theology is needed to stir the masses and save souls ; we defy all the negative theologians in England to give such proof of their ministry as we can. If we must be fools in glorying, we do, we must boast that the old doctrines are victorious, and that the Lord, the Spirit, has most signally honoured them. We do not cite the overwhelming and ever increasing multitudes who listen to us, as a proof in this matter, but, we do and will glory, in the power of the Gospel, in that it has brought so many to the cross of Christ, and raised so many from the dunghill. In every place where the old Gospel has been proclaimed it has had its trophies from the worst of men, and we are no exceptions to the rule. The slain of the Lord have been many. His arrows have found out the hearts of His enemies ; many have been overthrown by His Spirit, and have been ultimately brought to find life and healing in the blood of Jesus. The best evidences of the truth of our holy religion, are to be found in the marvellous effects it produces. Drunkards, harlots, swearers, thieves, liars, and such like, when reclaimed and regenerated, are the jewels in the crown of the truth ; of such we must say in confidence, ' What hath God wrought ? ' "—*Preface to Vol. II. of The New Park Street Pulpit.*

VII.

TWO THOUSAND PRINTED SERMONS.

CONCERNING their weekly publication, and concerning individual sermons, many remarkable things are told. Some on special topics have commanded a very extensive sale, the one on Baptismal Regeneration leading the way. When this was first published, it was feared that the circulation would be disastrously affected, but the number of subscribers actually increased.

The history of these sermons would constitute a unique chapter in the annals of the church. Some years ago, an ardent admirer of Mr. Spurgeon gave away, at his own charge, a quarter of a million copies. He had volumes elegantly bound for presentation to the crowned heads of Europe. He also had books, containing a dozen in each, sent to every member of both Houses of Parliament, and to all the students of Oxford and Cambridge. More singular still was their circulation " as advertisements in the Australian papers ; one gentleman spending week by week a sum which we scarcely dare to mention, lest it should not be believed." In a sense, Mr. Spurgeon is a preacher to the whole Protestant world ; and if any doubt this remarkable fact, let them note what he himself says about the general diffusion of these pulpit discourses :—

" In America the sale of the edition published there was extremely large, and I believe that it still continues ; but dozens of religious papers appropriate the sermons bodily, and, therefore, it is quite impossible to say where they go, or, rather, where they do not go. Of translations, the Dutch have been most plentiful, making large volumes. An edition of two volumes of selected sermons has been circulated in the colony of the Cape of Good Hope, among the Dutch settlers of that region. In German there are three noble volumes, besides many smaller ones. German publishers, with the exception of Mr. Oncken, of Hamburg, seldom have the courtesy to send the author a copy ; and I have picked up in divers places sermons bearing date from Baden, Basle, Carlsruhe, Ludwigsburg, and so on. How many, therefore, may have been sold in Germany I am unable to compute. In French several neat volumes have appeared ; in Welsh and Italian one volume each. In Sweden a handsome edition in four volumes has been largely circulated, and the translator informed me of the conversion of some of noble and even royal birth through their perusal. Besides these, there are single sermons in Spanish, Gaelic, Danish, Russ, Maori, Telugu, and some other tongues, and permission has been sought and gladly given for the production of a volume in the language of Hungary."

Did literature represent his sole profession, the fruits of Mr. Spurgeon's pen could not be expected to be more abundant than they are, even though the sermons be left out of the category. Authorship is to him a pleasure as well as a duty ; and he evidently values literary power as a sacred trust to be accounted for hereafter.

At the present date Mr. Spurgeon has published not far short of two thousand separate sermons in the regular weekly series, besides hundreds of others, so that the position he occupies as a popular preacher is not only extraordinary, but absolutely unique. There are volumes of sermons which have commanded, and still continue to command, a large sale ; there is not, however, another instance on record of a pastor's utterances attracting tens of thousands of purchasers through a third of a century. If we examine the quality of the earliest numbers of the series we shall see abundant reason for their instant popularity. By many, whose judgment is worthy of respect, these earliest productions are thought to be quite equal to anything which has followed. The glow of sanctified genius is on every page ; and the volumes are pervaded by the warm zeal and freshness of youth which are irresistible. Indeed, I have been told by a gentleman who heard the Pastor of the Tabernacle on the first day of his preaching in London, and who hears him still, that Mr. Spurgeon has never improved, nor has he ever grown in the sense that others grow——he was sent forth complete at first, just as Minerva was never a child, but sprang at once fully armed from the head of Jupiter. Though not prepared to acquiesce in such a judgment without some qualification, I think it is well to record it as a characteristic of a prevalent opinion. The pastor of a Nonconformist church might also be quoted, who considers that the earlier sermons are even superior to those of to-day.

Hence there was every prospect of the under-taking proving a commercial success when Mr. Joseph Passmore, at the close of the year 1854, proposed to the Pastor that a discourse should be issued regularly every week ; for long prior to his preaching days the idea had come uninvited into the mind of Mr. Spurgeon himself, that he would

" one day preach sermons which would be printed." It would appear that some time elapsed before the preacher even thoroughly believed in his own popularity. The sermons had sold in an unparalleled manner as occasional publications ; but when a shrewd, far-seeing publisher asked if the publication should be advanced into a weekly institution, the answer in the affirmative was given " with much fear and trembling."

In the preface to the first volume of the published discourses, dated January 1856, the remark occurs : " Little can be said in praise of these sermons, and nothing can be said against them more bitter than has been already spoken." The author also declares that he is " invulnerable either to criticism or abuse." The admission is then conceded that a departure has been ventured on " from the usual mode of preaching." An answer is also given to the question, What is Calvinism ? It is not a slavish adherence to the views of one man ; the word is rather a brief and convenient one to express " that salvation is by grace alone." There are things in the book which may provoke a smile, but what of them ? The preacher " is not quite sure about a smile being a sin, and, at any rate, he thinks it less crime to cause a momentary laughter than a half hour's profound slumber."

A little more than a year after Mr. Spurgeon's settlement at New Park Street a scheme was set on foot for the enlargement of the chapel, which was ultimately carried out at a cost of £2,000. On the last Sabbath of January 1855 a collection was made for this object. The text was, "Thou hast made us unto our God kings and priests." The inferences at the close were, "I am king, I will give as a king giveth unto a king." A priest, if he sacrificed, was not to give a maimed lamb or a blemished bullock. "Excuse my pressing this subject," the preacher continued. "I want to get this chapel enlarged ; we are all agreed about it ; we are all rowing in one boat. I have set my mind on £50, and I must and will have it to-day if possible. I hope you won't disappoint me." As a result of this appeal the people at once placed £50 in the plates held at the doors, and elevenpence halfpenny over.

On the 8th of July, 1855, while preaching at New Park Street from the words of the Psalmist, "He shall choose our inheritance for us," Mr. Spurgeon referred to the delights of hearing a sermon, which had for so long been denied to himself. He sometimes felt that he should occasionally like to sit down to the feast in God's house, and not always be a serving-man. "I am sure I should be glad to hear a sermon ; it is a

long time since I heard one ; but when I do
attend one it always tires me—I want to be
improving on it." His sermons were now being
published regularly ; he was preaching incessantly
in the week, so that the opportunities for hearing
were necessarily almost *nil.* At this time he had
not long completed his twentieth year.

According to his own confession, however,
Mr. Spurgeon this year saw and heard something
striking at Bristol. After coming away from
George Müller's Orphan House, he said, " I never
heard such a sermon in my life as I saw there."
When asked to address the children, he replied,
" I could not speak a word for the life of me." He
then received a lesson touching the power of faith
which bore abundant fruit ; and in connection with
this theme we have some first hints respecting
the Metropolitan Tabernacle. " I sometimes
think we will try the power of faith here," he
told his people on the first Sabbath evening in
November, " and see if we could not get sufficient
funds whereby to erect a place to hold the people
that crowd to hear the Word of God. We may
have a tabernacle of faith as well as an orphan-
house of faith."

The first volume of the sermons was reprinted
in America, and at once attained a circulation of
twenty thousand copies. This year, 1855, the

second of his ministry in London, he called "a year of miracles" in a sermon preached on December 30th; and among other causes for gratitude was the fact that two hundred and ten persons were added to the church, while others were coming in.

On the 6th of January, 1856, at New Park Street, he referred to his conversion, which had taken place exactly six years previously, and at that hour of the day. "Seeking rest and finding none," he said, "I stepped within the house of God, and sat there, afraid to look upward, lest I should be utterly cut off, and lest His fierce wrath should consume me. The minister rose in his pulpit, and as I have done this morning, read this text—'Look unto me, and be ye saved, all the ends of the earth; for I am God, and there is none else.' I looked that moment; the grace of faith was vouchsafed to me in the selfsame instant." *

Shortly after, or on the 10th of February, he preached on behalf of the Baptist Fund, an institution founded in London for the relief of poor ministers in 1717. Some of the illustrations of poverty were as sad as they were striking. Some ministers, when they ascended the pulpit stairs,

---

* As remarked elsewhere, the pulpit in which this sermon was preached is to be seen at the Stockwell Orphanage.

had to be careful lest they tore their worn-out
coats. The case of a preacher without means
was also mentioned, a man who walked twenty
miles and preached two sermons, and received
from the deacons a shilling for his services.
Another walked eight miles, found no one to give
him a dinner, preached three sermons, and was
rewarded with half-a-crown. The claims of the
Baptist Fund were strongly advocated.

On the first Sabbath of the November following,
Mr. Spurgeon preached at New Park Street for the
first time after the fatal accident at the Surrey
Gardens. He said that he almost regretted having
undertaken to preach, scarcely feeling equal to
the task. The text was Philippians ii. 9-11 :
" Wherefore God hath highly exalted him, and
given him a name which is above every name,"
etc.

This text, and the occasion of its being chosen,
became more than ever interesting when we are
further acquainted with the circumstances of the
case. Thus at the Pastors' College Conference,
held in April 1879, he mentioned a fact in connection with the accident at the Surrey Gardens
Music-Hall which is not generally known. He said
that the effect on his mind was such that he was
nearly imbecile for a fortnight. The newspapers
wrote as though he were responsible for the death

of the unfortunate people, and the slanders were almost more than he could bear. Such, too, was the agitation of his mind, joined to the assaults of Satan, that he seemed to lose the desire for prayer and for reading the Scriptures. He went away into the country ; and he related how relief came in an instant while walking in the garden of the house where he was staying. The words, " God hath given him a name," etc., flashed into his mind, and he seeing at once that all must be right, whatever the enemy might suggest, his joy was immediately as unspeakably great as his grief had previously been. He even went down on his knees on the gravel to give thanks.

After a storm of trial and persecution, the preface to the volume of sermons for 1857 strikes a more cheerful note. The preacher speaks of the winter being past and the spring-time of renewed vigour and peace having come. " The congregations during the year have been immense and enthusiastic," he says. " Our church meetings have been joyous occasions, for we have heard marvellous stories of profligates reclaimed, drunk- ards converted, and desponding souls delivered." He now realised that in the hands of God he was far more than the mere pastor of a church ; he seems to have felt that he was an evangelist raised up for a special work. Hence " the sermons preached at the music-hall are intended to arrest the attention of the careless, and alarm the consciences of the hardened. The reader will not, therefore, find in them that fulness and depth of doctrine which he may desire." It may be noted that on the 7th of October in this year Mr. Spurgeon preached at the Crystal Palace, Sydenham, to a congregation of twenty-four thousand people, the occasion "being the day appointed by Proclamation for a Solemn Fast, Humiliation, and Prayer before Almighty God : in order to obtain Pardon of our Sins, and for imploring His Blessing and Assistance on our Arms for the Restoration of Tranquillity in India."

The flow of success continued throughout the year 1858. The best results continued to arise from the reading of the sermons. "In lonely places there are churches of Christ whose only ministry is found in these pages, save when a passing evangelist is led to open his mouth among them," we are told. In rooms in the crowded haunts of poverty these are read to hundreds who could scarcely understand any language more refined ; while at races and fairs, and even at pilgrimages of the Romish church, these have been used by earnest brethren as a means of obtaining an audience in the open air." During this year the circulation of the sermons at home and abroad was more than sustained. No less than a hundred and fifty thousand volumes had already been sold in the United States ; in Australia more than one edition was printed, while translations appeared in several of the European languages, besides one in Welsh. In the meantime the weekly issue in London was as popular as ever.

Two providential deliverances occurred this year, which many will still remember. On Wednesday, the 7th of April, Mr. Spurgeon preached at Halifax, when, in consequence of a fall of snow and severe wintry weather, he did not anticipate meeting a very extensive congregation. A temporary building was erected, however, and from five to six thousand persons were found assembled. In the afternoon all went well ; but in the evening a gallery planned to hold two thousand people suddenly gave way after the service, when two persons were injured. "Now had this happened any earlier, not only must many have been injured," said Mr. Spurgeon to his congregation at the Surrey Gardens, "but there are a thousand chances to one, as we say, that a panic must necessarily have ensued, similar to that which we still remember and deplore as having occurred in this place. Had such a thing occurred, and had I been the unhappy preacher on the occasion, I feel certain that I should never have been able to occupy the pulpit again. Such was the effect of the first calamity that I marvel that I ever survived."

Six months later, or on the morning of October 10th, he appeared at the great music-hall, after having experienced in the week "excruciating pain and continual sickness." After this he was laid aside, and the next published number of the weekly sermon was one preached at Exeter Hall more than two years before. Though so old, the preacher prayed that the utterances might " bud afresh and bring forth fruit, even as old corn, after having been entombed in Egyptian sepulchres for centuries, will often germinate again and yield an abundant crop." For three weeks the issue of old sermons continued, and a letter from the Pastor appears in each. In one he refers to the timbers in his frail barque having been made to creak ; in another he speaks of the memorable panic of two years before. On the 7th of November he again occupied the pulpit.

In the course of the year 1859 several sermons were preached which were made wonderfully useful in awakening the careless. They continued to command a very extensive sale in America, and not only in a separate form but in the news-papers. Thus " in the midst of a mass of frivolity and romance the weekly sermon stands like an· ambassador in bonds, hopeful, nevertheless, that its free voice may overcome the discordant cries which try to drown its utterance."

On the 13th of March in this year, at the Surrey Gardens, Mr. Spurgeon referred to the opening of his ministry, and again preached from his first text: "It is about eight years since, as a lad of sixteen, I stood up for the first time in my life to preach the Gospel in a cottage to a handful of poor people who had come together for worship. I felt my own inability to preach, but I ventured to take this text, 'Unto you therefore which believe, He is precious.'"

Nos. 268, 269, and 270 of *The New Park Street Pulpit* are filled with an account of "the ceremony of laying the first stone of the new Tabernacle," which ceremony was performed by Sir S. M. Peto on the 16th of August. Many honoured brethren who graced that occasion by their presence have since gone home to heaven. There were two meetings, one on the ground in the afternoon, and one at Rea's Repository in the evening. "In the bottle which is to be placed under the stone we have put no money," remarked the Pastor, "for one good reason—we have none to spare. We have not put news-papers, because, albeit we admire and love the liberty of the press, yet that is not so immediately concerned in this edifice. The articles placed under the stone are simply these : the Bible, the Word of God—we put that as the foundation of the church. Upon this rock doth Christ build the ministration of His truth. We know of nothing else as our standard. Together with this we have put the old Baptist Confession of Faith which was signed in the olden times by Benjamin Keach, whose name is in this book. We put also the *declaration of the deacons*, which you have just heard read, printed on parchment. There is also an edition of Dr. Rippon's Hymn-Book printed just before he died ; and then, in the last place, there is a programme of this day's proceedings."

One of the speakers present at the evening meeting was Judge Payne, who, as a matter of course, composed a tailpiece, besides indulging in some sensible wit. " Now what does C. H. S. mean ? " he asked, glancing at one of the decorations. " Why, it means, first, Charles Haddon Spurgeon ; but *I* do not mean that. C. H. S. means a *Clear Headed Speaker*, who is *Clever* at *Handling Subjects* in a *Cheerful Hearted Style.* He is a *Captain* of the *Hosts* of *Surrey ;* he is a *Cold Hating Spirit;* he has *Chapel Heating Skill;* he is a *Catholic Humbug Smasher ;* he is a *Care-Hushing Soother ;* he is a *Child Helping*

14

Strengthener; he is a *Christ Honouring Soldier;* and he is *Christ's Honoured Servant.*"

At this meeting one of the most interesting speeches of the evening was made by the Pastor's father, the Rev. John Spurgeon, who also gave some reminiscences of his son's youthful days given elsewhere.

In 1860 Mr. Spurgeon felt the pressure of having to sustain a weekly publication. "No man can well conceive what a drain it is upon a preacher to have his sermons constantly printed," he remarked ; "he can scarcely hope to avoid repetition, and will be constantly in danger of running dry." Having preached for the last time at the Surrey Gardens on the 11th of December, 1859, he adds, "This sixth year saw us sorrowfully removing from the Surrey Music-Hall to a far less convenient spot." Individual sermons are mentioned which had been abundantly useful in the conversion of sinners, while the translation of the discourses into Swedish had very greatly increased the circulation.

The morning service was now conducted in Exeter Hall until the 3rd of June, when Mr. Spurgeon departed for the Continent on a brief tour. During his absence several sermons preached at New Park Street on Sabbath evenings appeared in the weekly issue. He appeared again at

Exeter Hall on the 29th of July; and on Tuesday, the 21st of August, gave an account of his continental tour to a large audience in the unfinished Tabernacle.

The year 1861 saw the presentation made of two hundred thousand copies of the Sermons to the Universities of Oxford and Cambridge. The discourses still continued to be published in numbers of American newspapers, while they were read from village pulpits in our own country. This was the year of the opening of the Tabernacle, and the preliminary services extended through a month. The first prayer-meeting was held at seven o'clock a.m., on Monday, the 18th of March; and on the afternoon of the Monday following Mr. Spurgeon preached his first sermon in the building, the text being Acts v. 42: "And daily in the temple, and in every house, they ceased not to teach and to preach Jesus Christ." In the volume of sermons for this year there are three which are not by Mr. Spurgeon, the preachers having been Messrs. Brock, Stowell Brown, and Octavius Winslow. On the afternoon and in the evening of April 11th, meetings were held for the Exposition of the Doctrines of Grace. After an introductory address by Mr. Spurgeon the following subjects were very ably handled by successive speakers. *Election:* Mr. J. Bloomfield.

Human Depravity : Mr. Evan Probert. *Particular Redemption :* Mr. J. A. Spurgeon. *Effectual Calling :* Mr. James Smith. *The Final Preservation of the Saints :* Mr. W. O'Neill. On the following evening Mr. Henry Vincent gave an oration in the chapel on *Nonconformity*, and this also appears in the volume of sermons.

In 1862 a friend scattered " a large number of sermons in the colleges and towns of Ireland. Working with great discretion, he sowed the seed so rapidly in each place that, before the foul bird, the Popish priest, could hasten to stop him, the work was done."

On the 30th of January Mr. Spurgeon preached on the Hartley Colliery Accident, from the words of Job. xiv. 14, "If a man die, shall he live again ?" The evening was wet and cold ; but the people nevertheless mustered in force, and the sum of £120 was collected for the relief fund. On the 9th of November he also preached on behalf of the distress in Lancashire.

In consequence of the abolition of the duty on paper, the sermons commenced appearing in large type in the opening of 1862. The last of the small type series has a mourning border, having been preached on the occasion of the death of the good Prince Consort.

During the year 1863 a mention is made of

the friends who send texts for the Pastor to handle. "This we cannot engage to do," he says. " Our habit has been to look to the Lord for our guidance, and when a text comes with power to our soul we preach from it without hesitation ; but as we dare not select our own themes, so neither can we receive those suggested to us, unless our Master sends them upon our heart."

The following year was the era of the great Baptismal Regeneration controversy, and the fact is mentioned that at the close of the year the sermons on the question of baptism had reached a circulation of 300,000. The principal discourse was preached on the 5th of June ; and the controversy awakened may still be estimated by the scores of pamphlets which were published on both sides. Before this storm had subsided the Pastor dropped " The Reverend " as a ministerial title. It appears for the last time on the sermon number 587, and preached on August 28th. In the following week, and ever since, the name is printed simply, C. H. Spurgeon.

In the preface to the Sermons for 1865 it is said that the " weekly circulation has during the past year been fully maintained," " while proofs of usefulness are as numerous and encouraging as ever." With January of this year commenced *The Sword and the Trowel,* which at once did great service to the cause nearest the Editor's heart. Towards the end of the year there appeared a notice of a bazaar to be held in the Tabernacle, the proceeds to be devoted to the work of chapel building in London. " From the success already achieved," said Mr. Spurgeon, " I am encouraged to attempt yet greater things, and to seek the erection, during the year 1866, of several new buildings." Just at this time a pamphlet, which has long since been forgotten, occasioned the Pastor some annoyance. He was compelled to give notice that he had not written the *brochure*, and that he was shocked at the manner in which a professed minister of the Gospel had employed his name to give weight to prophecies which were ridiculous ravings.

With the close of his twelfth volume in 1866 the preacher rejoiced in the thought that he was still teaching the same Old Gospel with which he had commenced. " Our twelve volumes, like the sons of Jacob, can say, ' we are all one man's sons, we are true men.' In fundamentals we remain like the oak, rooted to the same soil, although in circumstantials here and there a branch spreads itself otherwise than it did ten years ago. Growth there should be, but not wanton change." Now we begin to see the first notice of the Colportage Association. Persons disposed to aid the new

scheme were reminded of the " sellers of trinkets,"
who ages ago on the Continent carried the Bible
in their packs as " the best of jewels " ; and of the
pedlars who in the seventeenth century carried
the best books of the Puritans throughout England.   It was at this time also that Mr. Spurgeon
appeared for the first time among the Quakers.
" Our belief was, and still is," he said, " that it
is the bounden duty of the Society of Friends in
these perilous times to renew more distinctly their
testimony against formalism, ritualism, and un-
spiritual worship in its many forms, and we hoped
that a respectful brotherly admonition might be
accepted by them and owned of God."   On the
6th of November he addressed a gathering of
twelve hundred Friends at their head-quarters in
Bishopsgate, feeling at the time much physical
pain, and weighed down with a sense of responsibility.

After six years' wear and tear, the Tabernacle
was renovated in the spring of 1867, and Mr.
Spurgeon preached to vast congregations in the
Islington Agricultural Hall, on five consecutive
Sabbath mornings.   The volume of sermons for
1867 was the last which contained a preface ; and
as the succeeding volumes come more within the
recollection of readers than those noticed, there is
no need to continue these jottings.   The circula-

tion is still maintained, and the crowds attracted to the Tabernacle show no signs of diminution. As Mr. Spurgeon is only fifty-two, it may be supposed that, according to the ordinary course of nature, he has much of the best part of life before him. Let friends far and near unite to pray that physical strength may be granted to the preacher who has been chosen of God for the accomplishment of great things, and whose enforced inactivity is a real loss to the church.

*THE PREACHER'S REWARD—ANECDOTES
ABOUT THE SERMONS.*

"What is the crown of a church? Well, some churches have one crown, and some another. I have heard of a church whose crown was its organ—the biggest organ, the finest organ ever played, and the choir the most wonderful choir that ever was. Everybody in the district said, ' Now if you want to go to a place where you will have fine music that is the spot.' Our musical friends may wear that crown if they please. I will never pluck at it or decry it ; I feel no temptation in that direction. I have heard of others whose crown has been their intellect. There are very few people indeed, not as many people by one-tenth as there are sittings, but then they are such a select people, the *élite*, the thoughtful and intelligent ! The ministry is such that only one in a hundred can possibly understand what is said, and the one in the hundred who does understand it, is therefore a most remarkable person. That is their crown. Again I say I will not filch it. What-ever there may be that is desirable about it, the brother who wears it, shall wear it all his days for me. I have heard of other crowns ; amongst the rest, that of being ' a most respectable church.' All the people are respectable. The minister of course is respectable. I believe he is ' Reverend,' or, ' Very Reverend,' and everybody and thing about him is to the last degree ' respectable.' Fustian jackets and cotton gowns are warned off by the surpassing dignity of everything in and around the place. As for a working man, such a creature is never seen on the premises, and could not be supposed to be ; and if he were to come he would say, ' The preacher preaches double Dutch or Greek, or some-thing of the sort ; he would not hear language he could understand. This is not a very brilliant crown—this crown of respectability : it certainly never flashed ambition into my soul. But our crown under God has been this,—the poor have the Gospel preached unto them, souls are saved, and Christ is glorified."—*Memorial of Silver Wedding Testi-monial*, pp. 23, 24.

VIII.

ONE of the peculiarities of the preaching of Whitefield was the large number of persons who would be convicted of sin under one sermon ; but in the case of Mr. Spurgeon we have to take into account the world-wide audience which, through the printed sermons, he is always addressing. With his matchless voice, the great preacher of the last century may have been able to deliver his message to some twenty or thirty thousand persons ; but that was a small number indeed when compared with the hundreds of thousands in the Old and the New World, and at the antipodes, who, as may be said, make up Mr. Spurgeon's regular congregation. Then, in addition to the English-speaking race, the sermons are also being read in many foreign languages· into which they have been translated. The position occupied by the preacher is thus quite unique, nothing like it ever having been known

before.   During some years past instances of usefulness of the printed sermons, under the head of
" Personal Notes," have appeared in *The Sword
and the Trowel*, and from these we borrow our
illustrations for the present chapter.

We suppose that the examples of enemies
tamed have been many ; but one striking instance
of this kind· was that of a gentleman who was
greatly prejudiced against Mr. Spurgeon, and
dissenters generally, until he visited the Metropolitan Tabernacle, which visit was brought about
in a somewhat remarkable manner.   " Some time
after my conversion I came to London," says the
son of this gentleman.   " A few weeks later my
father was up for a few days, and wishing to
see me, I proposed Sunday morning as my only
convenient time, and the Metropolitan Tabernacle
as a midway meeting-place.   I so arranged that
we met there just as the crowds were flocking
into the building.   As I guessed would be the
case, seeing such crowds pressing in, my father
could not resist the temptation to follow."   The
result was that he was greatly affected by the
sermon—" Deep calleth unto deep," No. 865—
and from being an enemy of the preacher the
astonished hearer was changed into one of Mr.
Spurgeon's most steadfast friends.   " I am thankful to testify," added his son, " that what light

and peace he had came through the Metropolitan Tabernacle sermons."

On one occasion a thank-offering of £5, which came to the College funds, is connected with the welcome story of the conversion of a prodigal. The father of the young man in question derived some consolation from a sermon by Mr. Spurgeon on the Prodigal Son, and he sent a request that the youth might be prayed for at the ordinary Monday evening prayer-meeting. The prayer was answered, the young man became a changed character ; and the joy of the father found vent in the giving of the thank-offering mentioned.

Probably it is a great joy to the Pastor to know that his discourses are frequently a source of great joy to the very poor among his flock. A friend who visits in a certain village of Middlesex tells of an old needlewoman who could not attend public worship regularly. At the best she was not able to earn more than a sorry pittance ; but nevertheless, when on a Saturday night she would find herself with no more than threepence to last until Monday, she would still spare a penny for the weekly sermon, after buying what bread and tea she could obtain for two-pence. What kind of satisfaction she found in the perusal of the weekly numbers was seen in her confession, to the effect that when she got into the cream of the sermon she would not change places with the Queen herself. She was often so interested that she would even forget to eat her bread; but at the same time her solicitude for others was so great, that when the numbers accumulated she went abroad to distribute them, so that others might share the blessing with herself.

When the Hants Congregational Union met at Bournemouth in 1881, a deacon who was present enlivened the proceedings by narrating the following : " About seven years since a poor woman had saved up a few pounds of money and was going into the town of Christchurch to purchase some things. By some means she lost her purse, which contained a five-pound note, one pound in gold, and some fourteen shillings in silver. She was much distressed at her loss, and had some hand-bills circulated offering a reward for the restoration of her property. A person found the purse and appropriated the whole of its contents, and nothing has been heard of the affair until a fortnight since, when a gentleman went to the printer of the handbill and asked if he could remember the incident. On looking over his file he saw the bill, and the whole of the circumstances came to his mind. The gentleman then said, ' You must ask me no questions, but the purse will be restored.' A few days afterwards the identical purse, with the amount of money lost, and £3 for interest, was sent to the rightful owner. *The cause which brought this about was reading Spurgeon's Sermons.*"

There was a youth who died in 1881 who had always been an invalid ; and who just before his death settled his little money accounts, apportioning £40 to Mr. Spurgeon's work. " As you will suppose," wrote a relative to the Pastor in September 1881, " he has been for some time taking an interest in your work for Christ, and one of the greatest enjoyments of his life was the hearing you preach one Sunday last spring. He has read your sermons, etc., for a long time, and distributed them among our poor neighbours. His life has been one of much suffering, chiefly from asthma; but now consumption is carrying him off, and he is lying in the most peaceful, tranquil state, waiting the Master's call." The sufferer said he should value a word from Mr. Spurgeon ; but although the Pastor wrote by return of post his interesting correspondent died before the letter could reach him.

Among the converts from Ritualism a case occurred of a young man who yielded to the seductions of that Romanising sect after he had been educated as a nonconformist. He became a

thorough Anglican, he even went to confession to
his vicar ; but when disease set in and showed him
that he must shortly leave the present world, he
found that the specious doctrines of his new friends
would not do, and probably he had never very
sincerely believed in them.   Of course he had
heard of Mr. Spurgeon ; and having expressed a
desire to see some of his works, the wish was very
readily complied with, and the invalid then found
what he wanted.   A Christian friend also conversed with him, until at last the young man
showed the possession of a triumphant faith,
and so he died.

A friend who happened to be travelling through
Nottingham was asked to visit a dying woman at
a public-house ; but instead of wanting any instruction or consolation, the woman was found to
be rejoicing in Christ ; and on being asked how
she had found such peace, she showed a piece of
torn newspaper containing a passage from one
of Mr. Spurgeon's Sermons, and which had come
with a parcel from Australia.   " Talk about the
hidden life of the good seed ! " remarked the
friend referred to.   " Think of that sermon
preached in London, conveyed to America, an
extract reprinted in a newspaper there, that
paper sent to Australia, part then torn off (as we
should say accidentally), the parcel dispatched to

England, and, after all its wanderings, conveys the message of salvation to the woman's soul. God's Word shall not return to Him void."

An evangelist to whom the sermons were supplied gratuitously by a friend thus shows how the numbers may be widely distributed in a country district: "I know a baker in Norfolk, and to him I send some to distribute among the poor families to whom he delivers his bread, as he goes through the village with his cart. In the same way, by post and other means, to other individuals, as to so many centres, getting them to lend them from house to house amongst their neighbours. I make a few sermons reach a wide circle, chiefly among those who else would never see them. Nor has this been without results, as I have from time to time intimated. Scores have felt in a measure what one woman experienced from reading one ; it gave her so much comfort that she told me she had read it a hundred times, and that with undiminished pleasure, and wore it in her bosom until she tore it to tatters."

Of the manner in which the sermons are read by the clergy, and also used by them to good purpose, is shown by Mrs. Spurgeon in her work on the Book Fund ; but of course many other examples might be given. Thus, in one instance, a certain evangelical clergyman, who was quite as

15

useful as he was popular, accidentally left his bag at a country railway-station in Kent. The railway authorities looked into the bag, as they are accustomed to do, in order to discover, if possible, some trace of ownership ; but on this occasion no revelation was forthcoming beyond what could be given by a number of marked and otherwise well-used copies of Mr. Spurgeon's sermons. In due time a telegram arrived to ask the stationmaster to kindly forward the bag to its reverend owner, who possibly would have continued his useful labours with more difficulty had the bag been irrecoverably lost.

Our friends in the North have ever regarded Mr. Spurgeon as one of their most favourite divines ; and thus I will now give some facts illustrative of the work of the sermons in Scotland.

In 1881 a certain fisherman sent to the Pastor a very pleasantly-told account of his conversion : " I remember a colporteur coming to my mother's house, and he asked me if I would buy a book," our northern friend remarks. " ' Yes,' says I, ' if you have got any ballads, that is, Scotch songs.' So he says to me, ' If you give me a piece of fish I will give you something that will do you more good than ballads.' I saw he desired my good, so I gave him half a codfish, and he gave me one of your sermons. The text was, ' Look unto

Me and be ye saved, all the ends of the earth ; for I am God and there is none else.' (" Sovereignty and Salvation," No. 60.) While reading that sermon the blessed Spirit of God enlightened my understanding, and I saw Jesus set before me as my Saviour. Blessed hour ! Happy day ! Jesus washed my sins away."

On one occasion a certain pastor lost himself in one of the Highland glens ; he found the natives to be a kindly race, and although they had little notion of either Lord Beaconsfield or Mr. Gladstone, they were extremely familiar with the name of Spurgeon. " They had a sort of knowledge of that name, for they read your sermons, and fetched a lot out to show me that they did so," remarked the pastor referred to. " I assure you," he adds, " I never saw any man's works with such signs of use upon them. There was no kirk in the glen, so on Sundays they got together and had a service, the scholar of the place reading the sermon." One aged pilgrim declared he would go to Glasgow on his hands and knees to see the preacher ; and though hardly competent to walk as many yards without effort, as it was miles to the commercial metropolis, the light in his eye bespoke his intense earnestness.

On the little island called the Skerries Rock there is a lighthouse, and, including the keepers of this, there were in all sixteen individuals in the place ; and having no church they can go to, they are accustomed to conduct a service for themselves on the Lord's Day. "Thus," says *The Free Church Monthly* for December 1882, "the words to which thousands in London listen every week, and which are read in every corner of the world, are feeding and comforting the sixteen inhabitants of a lonely rock, beaten by the fierce waters that surge in the Pentland Firth."

While staying at a certain health-resort, a kind-hearted friend laid a number of the sermons on the table of the coffee-room at the hotel ; but while many were pleased to have an opportunity of reading the numbers, there was a certain "stiff aged churchman" who protested against the introduction of "the works of a man who cursed our church." Then a Christian lady came to the help of the Quakeress, telling how both she and her husband prized the sermons highly, and how useful they had been in a district at Aberdeen. In that city there had dwelt a soldier "whose hardened, wretched condition baffled all the Christian labours bestowed upon him, until she lent him 'Only Trust Him' (No. 1635)," when that became instrumental in his conversion. Then " Jesus Only " (No. 924) had proved equally useful in the case of a Romanist, a most miserable

being, who till that moment was placing her
dependence in confession and penance. The
transformation of both of these was described as
having been really remarkable. Still more striking,
however, was the change which came over the
venerable churchman after the lady who had
given these instances had departed. He even
allowed his Quaker friend to read to him the
sermons which had proved so useful, and remarked, " The venom is passing away. I feel it
going. I shall buy those sermons and send
them to my Broad Church son, and I hope they
will do him and his wife good, and that he will
preach them in his church." The gentleman
went even so far as to confess that the discourses
had " softened an old rebel." This is a memorable
instance of the power of the Word.

When he was in Scotland in the summer of
1883, Mr. Spurgeon heard of many instances of
usefulness through the sermons, especially in lonely
Highland districts. " In one far-away village in
the north," it is remarked, " the little country
shop is opened on Saturdays expressly for the
sale of the sermons ; and what the customers
want is so clearly understood, that often not a
word is spoken by either buyer or seller, but the
people walk in, put down the penny, and march
off with the sermon that is to be their Sabbath

feast.   In a Convalescent Home every Sabbath
evening during the winter the matron reads one
of the sermons to the inmates, who appear to be
very grateful for them."

Not very long ago, or in 1884, one of Mr.
Spurgeon's evangelists gave a very telling anecdote : " A woman in Scotland who was determined,
as far as possible, not to have anything to do
with religion, threw her Bible, and all the tracts
she could find in her house, into the fire.   One
of the tracts fell down out of the flames, so she
picked it up and thrust it in again.   A second time
it slipped down, and once more she put it back.
Again her evil intention was frustrated, but the
next time she was more successful, though even
then only half of it was consumed.   Taking up
the portion that fell out of the fire she exclaimed,
' Surely the devil is in that tract, for it won't burn ! '
Her curiosity was excited ; she began to read it,
and it was the means of her conversion.   The
' tract ' was one of the sermons published in *The
Metropolitan Tabernacle Pulpit.*   Verily, that sermon, and the woman too, were *saved, yet so as
by fire.*"

The above instances sufficiently testify to the
popularity of the sermons in Scotland ; but according to the witness of a certain Methodist minister,
who wrote in 1880, the discourses are equally

valued in some parts of Ireland. " Many a time these few years I have wondered whether you know that you are preaching in unnumbered pulpits every Lord's Day, in many cases word for word as reported in your volumes," remarks this friend in a letter to Mr. Spurgeon. " You are aware, I suppose, that the weekly sermon is read by two-thirds of the Protestants in Ulster? In some cases ten families join in taking it, and lend it from one to another." After this we need not wonder that the Protestants of Ulster should regard Mr. Spurgeon as their adviser-in-general, even on political matters ; and that they should have asked his opinion in regard to Home Rule when they were threatened with Mr. Gladstone's innovations.

We believe it was a Welsh dame who remarked, that if he only wanted one of his eyes Mr. Spurgeon would be worthy to come after Christmas Evans; but be that as it may, the preacher's utterances are as well calculated to be useful in Wales as elsewhere. In one instance, at least, the good which a couple of young men derived from the reading of the sermons did not end with themselves. They were encouraged to begin a Sabbath-school, and having commenced in two cottages with five scholars, they soon wanted more room, and they progressed until at length they were enabled to put up a building in which between two and three hundred children could be taught at once. Beyond this, they took care to circulate more than eighty copies of the sermons every week.

At Bryher, which is one of the Scilly Isles, the hundred and twenty persons who make up the population have a chapel as well as a church for their accommodation; and when service is held in the one place the custom is for the other to be closed. In 1880, when the intelligence was received, it was a usual thing for the sexton and clerk of the church to read one of Mr. Spurgeon's sermons in the chapel, and then to give out Wesley's Hymns for the little congregation to sing, when the Anglican establishment was closed.

The circulation of the sermons in the United States is very large, for not only are separate volumes issued, the newspapers appropriate each weekly issue as their own, so that the general diffusion is more widespread than can very readily be realized. It is quite possible that the readers are even more numerous in the United States than they are in the United Kingdom. It will be remembered by many that some years ago an enterprising American undertook to telegraph each Sunday morning sermon across the Atlantic, in order that the readers in more than one

American city might read on Monday morning what was spoken at the Metropolitan Tabernacle on the day before.

A letter received by Mr. Spurgeon in 1880 shows how his utterances may convey comfort as well as instruction into the most out-of-the-way corners of the American continent. " Several weeks ago I lay ill, far away from London, in the wilds of Florida," remarks the writer. " Weak and faint-hearted, I lay pondering on the strange providence of the Master, when one of your sermons was placed in my hands. The refreshing shower revived me and gave me fresh hope and courage, and I rose from my sick couch to strive still more earnestly to gain access to the hearts of those by whom I am surrounded, and to-day, in a small class that I have formed out here in the wilderness, the Lord made His presence felt, and blessed us with an awakening that I have never seen here before, and tears of repentance were shed by many. I am so full of joy and gratitude to God that I felt, indeed I longed, to let you know that your influence as an instrument had even reached this place."

Thus, the influence seems to reach to the very ends of the earth, and the personal testimony of one friend is frequently outdone by that of another. Thus, in 1881, a pastor in Tennessee

made this confession : " Nine years ago I was
a wild young man, but I was converted through
reading one of Mr. Spurgeon's sermons, and I am
now the minister of a large and influential church.
The Lord's name be magnified ! "

The tidings which come from the Far West
are no less cheering.   Writing to Mr. Spurgeon in
1882, a correspondent in Minnesota said :—" You
will be pleased to hear that in this Western
country, and in this village of six hundred inhabitants, Mr. Spurgeon's books are much valued.   I
have seen them in several houses here.   In the
Wesleyan minister's a volume or two of sermons.
In another house *Morning By Morning.*   In
another, that of an old saint, *The Saint and His
Saviour,* which he esteems as very precious, saying,
with emphatic tone, when he speaks of it, ' This is
Mr. Spurgeon's first book, and he has written
many since, but never one to surpass this,' though
the dear old man has not read a tithe of Mr.
Spurgeon's publications."

In 1884, the editor of a paper published in
New York, in which Mr. Spurgeon's sermons are
regularly issued, sent word to England that he
had recently heard of several remarkable cases in
which desperately wicked characters had abandoned
their ways through reading the Pastor's discourses.
Particular reference is made to an exceptionally

wicked character : " One aged reprobate, sixty years old, died last week, whose last two years were in startling contrast to all his past life. The transformation was the wonder of the neighbourhood for its completeness. From being a public terror he became a public blessing, as gentle and as kind as a woman. He was delivered from drunkenness, profanity, unchastity, and bloodshedding." On his death-bed this man desired that Mr. Spurgeon might be told of the grateful change which his sermons had been instrumental in effecting.

In 1882 the widow of the murdered President Garfield wrote to Mr. Spurgeon : " It is a choice treasure from my storehouse of beautiful memories that I sat beside General Garfield in the Metropolitan Tabernacle one bright summer Sunday morning (August 4th, 1867), and listened to your voice. I have this morning re-read from his journal the account of that day. A sentence from it may interest you. After describing very fully his impressions of the great audience, of the preacher, and of the sermon, he closes thus :—
' God bless Spurgeon ! He is helping to work out the problem of religious and civil freedom for England in a way that he knows not of.' "

In 1880 a young Scotchman, who died of anincurable disease in the General Hospital at

Montreal, gave a fine testimony to the influence
of Mr. Spurgeon's sermons; and a Christian
friend who visited him in his last illness sent an
account of the case to one of the journals of the
city :—" The one and only matter of his reading,
next to the Bible, was Charles H. Spurgeon's
sermons : of these he never tired. Biographies
of eminent Scotchmen like Norman Macleod and
William Arnot were taken to him, but as he put
them aside he would say, ' Spurgeon is always
the same, but always satisfying, for he makes
you forget himself, as he holds up Him who
is fairer than the children of men.' "   The
preacher's works find ready acceptance in Canada,
where the Pastors' College has a separate Association.

To come back to the Continent of Europe, we
find that the sermons even have readers among
the fishermen of the Mediterranean. A lady tells
of an adventure which happened in 1883, and
which shows in what sense this is true. While
staying at Cette, on the French coast, she went
out with a party in a boat on the sea, but in
consequence of an adverse gale the craft would
have been driven out until their lives would have
been endangered had not an Italian fisherman in
a sailing-boat gone to the rescue. Subsequently,
the fisherman called at the hotel accompanied

by his uncle; and the latter explained that, although they were Roman Catholics, he had the New Testament in French and English as well as in his own language—and he was a reader of Mr. Spurgeon's sermons.

Many of the so-called Reformed Churches in Switzerland need a second reformation, and this might well be brought about by a wider diffusion of Mr. Spurgeon's works among the people. In 1881, a young lady who applied for baptism to a Baptist minister in England gave a brief account of her history, and showed that she was a representative example of the wants of the country. Here is her testimony :—" My parents were members of the Protestant Established Church in Switzerland ; but though I attended the ordinancies, and observed the ceremonies, I always felt that I was a hypocrite, for I never believed in them, but desired something which I could never get in the Church. When I came to England I read a sermon by Mr. Spurgeon which did me good. *John Ploughman's Talk*, though funny, was made a great blessing to me. I then bought his sermons, and read them, and I am now happy to say that I am trusting in Jesus. When I return home I shall distribute these sermons, which have been so blessed to me." Thus the reading of the discourses tends to the multiplication of distributors, so that the good influence never ceases to extend.

Perhaps, on the whole, the Gospel is preached more fully in Denmark than in the once favoured and beautiful land where the Reformation found a refuge ; but even in the picturesque and out-of-the-way corners of Northern Europe Mr. Spurgeon's sermons, translated into the vernacular, are doing good service. By way of illustration take this characteristic note which a worthy Dane sent to the preacher in 1880 : —" Through twelve of your sermons, which are translated into Danish, I and my household have this winter been acquainted with your Christian announcement, and we thank you for every clearing and edifying word. We seceded from the Established Church a year ago, because we have so evidently seen the tragical consequences of the connection between the Church and the State, and we could not possibly act contrary to the conviction forced upon us by the New Testament, viz., the incorrectness of the infant baptism." The denomination which Mr. Spurgeon represents has obtained a very respectable footing in Denmark ; for although the population is under two millions, who for the most part are Lutherans, the Baptists are able to muster between three and four thousand members.

The vast empire of Russia, needing the

Scriptures in a great number of languages, is no small world in itself. Early in this century, when the Bible Society began its great mission, the pious Emperor Alexander was a leading patron of the work ; and although religion was checked in its progress during the ascendency of Nicolas, there has since been a revival of activity, the circulation of Mr. Spurgeon's sermons being also one of the signs of the times. Writing in 1881 to Mr. Spurgeon, a minister stationed at St. Petersburg says : " By your sermons, etc., you are having a part in the great work of spreading Christ's kingdom both in St. Petersburg and in the interior. You are well known among the priests, who seem to get hold of your translated sermons, and, strange to say, I know cases in which the Censor has readily given consent for your works to be translated when he has been reluctant respecting many." Another friend in the Russian capital made it his business to circulate as many of the translated copies as he could procure, the priests apparently being the most eager recipients.

Another friend in Russia, who wrote in 1880, says : " I came to this country about twenty-four years ago, and have been about in various parts of the interior ever since. . . I have a wife and eight children. A few weeks ago I explained to them

the meaning of the Orphanage, and appealed to
their feelings ; the result was that I was authorised
to go to their savings-bank and take out three
roubles forty kopecks as the children's contribution.
We have now made up the sum to fifty-five
roubles, which will be forwarded to you from St.
Petersburg by a cheque."

In the more remote parts of the Czar's vast
empire Mr. Spurgeon's works are not only known,
but are promoting the spiritual enlightenment of
the people in a way no less striking than gratify-
ing. Writing to the Pastor from Warschaw in
1882, Mr. F. H. Newton, of the German Baptist
Mission, thus refers to his adventures : " I have
during the last few weeks been visiting a number
of our Baptist Churches in Silesia and Russian
Poland ; and I think you will be interested to hear
of their activity and Christian faith. In almost
every town and village one of the first enquiries
put to me is, *And how is Brother Spurgeon ?*
In many of the outlying stations, where no stated
missionary can be sustained, your printed sermons
are regularly made use of : and I am sure you
will be thankful to our one Master to learn that
here in Poland, and elsewhere, many of the Church
members attribute their first religious awakening
to hearing some of those sermons read. In the
meetings which I have conducted in various towns

during this tour, I have frequently taken the opportunity of referring to the work of God which you are carrying on in London and elsewhere; and I have thought it only right to tell you of the warm and frequent salutations that are entrusted to me for yourself from our poor and out-of-the-way Baptist brethren in these parts. They especially rejoice to learn that your sons are also preaching the Word, and are particularly interested in the Book Fund established by Frau Spurgeon."

Labrador is an interesting country, not only on account of its brief charming summers and terrible winters. The people are mainly Roman Catholics, one reason being that a mission of that sect is maintained in the country. In 1884 a New York paper contained this piece of intelligence: —" All last winter, in the little mission on the Labrador coast, Mr. Spurgeon's sermons were read in the Mission Church, Sunday by Sunday, by the lady teachers, who were left by themselves for eight months, through the failing health of the devoted missionary who laboured there for many years. These simple services on the Sunday and weekday evenings, when these sermons were the staple of the teaching given, were greatly blessed by God. Many sailors came from the ships anchored off the coast, and, with the resident

16

fishermen, eagerly listened to the Word of Life, and not only were their hearts cheered and comforted, but some were brought to a knowledge of the truth as it is in Christ Jesus."

One distributor of the sermons among the natives of the Falkland Islands found that they were very thankfully received; and in 1880 a somewhat remarkable letter was received from a Red Kaffir, who resided at Port Elizabeth, South Africa. Being full of joy and peace, the man explained how the transformation had been effected: "One day as I was going to my daily work I met a friend of mine in the street. We spoke about the Word of God, and he asked me whether I had ever seen one of Mr. Spurgeon's books. I said, 'What Mr. Spurgeon is that—one of the Independent ministers in London?' and I said, 'No, I never saw such a book in my life.' He said he bought it from the bookseller. I asked the name of the book, and he said it was *The Metropolitan Tabernacle Pulpit*, and I went straight to the shop and bought one. I have read a good bit of it. . . . I am sure I can't tell how to describe the goodness you have done to us, the black people of South Africa. We are not black only outside, even inside; I wouldn't mind to be a black man only in colour. It is a terrible thing to be a black man from the soul to the skin ; but still I am very glad to say your sermons have done something good to me."

Two missionaries labouring in Greece once testified to Mr. Spurgeon : " Your sermons are to us like rain upon a dry land. We have no church to attend, and no friends to associate with." Similar testimony in regard to the great assistance received from the printed sermons comes from South Australia. In 1881 Pastor Thomas Spurgeon, of Auckland, enclosed a piece of *The Melbourne Argus*, which contained the sermon No. 735—" Loving Advice for Anxious Seekers," with this explanation, addressed to his mother : " This scrap of newspaper has been given to me by a town missionary here, who regards it as a very precious relic. It came to him from a man who died in the hospital, and bequeathed it to his visitor as a great treasure. The man found it on the floor of a hut in Australia, and was brought by its perusal to a knowledge of the truth as it is in Jesus. He kept it carefully while he lived (for it was dis-coloured and torn when he found it), and on his death-bed he gave it to the missionary as the only treasure he had to leave behind him. I thought dear father might like to have it in his book ; if not, send it back to me, that I may return it to its owner, who says he often feels encouraged by glancing at it. It was his desire, however, that I should send it home, that the dear preacher might be encouraged."

There was a certain Christian gentleman who had some of the sermons inserted in the Australian newspapers, himself paying the heavy cost. The above may have been one of these insertions. Another instance was that of a shepherd, who read a sermon in one of the journals while looking after his sheep, and the truth reached his heart. After his conversion he asked a clergyman, who was holding services at a gold-field, to give him Christian work ; and after beginning as a Sunday-school teacher, he went on till he became himself a preacher to gold-diggers.

As it is on the mainland, so is it in the islands of the Australasian world. The wife of a pastor in Tasmania once said, in a letter to her father : " If Mr. Spurgeon knew how his sermons are appreciated in our southern forests, where no preachers have been for years until my dear husband went to them, and how many cases of conversion he met with through the reading of them, he would be amazed, and rejoice with unspeakable joy."

The sermons are also read in India, many educated natives, including even some Brahmans, finding great pleasure in the persual. Having had presented to him No. 1500 of *The Metropolitan Tabernacle Pulpit*, a Brahman B.A. of Madras University wrote this critique on the discourse, and sent it to a friend : " The few minutes I have been reading these sermons daily were spent very agreeably. I always considered Dr. Spurgeon the best orator. I see even the best can improve ; as Dr. Spurgeon excels all orators, so his 1500th sermon excels all his other sermons. I doubt very much whether he himself can deliver such another sermon, but that is going too far. I envy those that hear personally Dr. Spurgeon preach."

In another instance a Christian lady lent a volume of the sermons to a Mahometan, and some time after was rewarded by receiving the following note : " Your sermon book has, indeed, converted me to Christianity. I do believe in Christ our Lord, and so long as my belief in Him is firmly rooted, I do not care what I may be called in the outer world. Mr. Spurgeon appears to be an extraordinary man." No one who properly apprehends the situation can doubt that, in proportion as the Gospel extends in our vast Indian empire, the circulation of these sermons will also extend.

The sermons are also found on the sea ; and many during a season of enforced leisure find in

them the truth that reaches the heart. Not very
long ago Mr. A. G. Brown told his people this
story of a conversion through reading while on
the ocean :—

" There came to me here one day a grand-
looking fellow. I had not to ask whether he
did business on the water, for the sea-breeze had
kissed his brow so often that it had left its mark
there. I said, ' Where did you find the Lord ? '
In a moment he answered, ' *Latitude* 25, *Longitude* 54.' I confess that rather puzzled me. I
had heard of people finding Jesus Christ in these
galleries, and down these aisles, and in all sorts
of places, but here was something quite different.
' Latitude 25, Longitude 54 ! What do you
mean ? ' He said, ' I was sitting on deck, and
out of a bundle of papers before me I pulled one
of Spurgeon's sermons. I began to read it. As
I read it I saw the truth, and I received Jesus
in my heart. I jumped off the coil of ropes
saved. I thought if I were on shore I would
know where I was saved, and why should I not
know on the sea ? And so I took my latitude
and longitude.' "

The sermons thus reach all classes ; and not
only are they instrumental in the conversion of
sinners, large numbers of Christian people are
by their perusal built up in the faith. The

audience addressed week by week is truly a world-wide one.

At the outset of his career in London, and while preaching at New Park Street Chapel on October 7th, 1855, Mr. Spurgeon himself referred to the extended influence he was even then beginning to exercise on the world through the press, *e.g.* :—

"Oh to think that we may write and print books which shall reach poor sinners' hearts! The other day my soul was gladdened exceedingly by an invitation from a pious woman to go and see her. She told me she had been ten years on her bed, and had not been able to stir from it. 'Nine years,' she said, 'I was dark' and blind, and unthinking; but my husband brought me one of your sermons. I read it, and God blessed it to the opening of my eyes. He converted my soul with it. And now—all glory to Him—I love His name! Each Sabbath morning,' she said, 'I wait for your sermon. I live on it all the week, as marrow and fatness to my spirit.' Ah! thought I, there is something to cheer the printers, and all of us who labour in that good work. One good brother wrote to me this week, 'Brother Spurgeon, keep your courage up. You are known in multitudes of households of England, and you are loved too;

though we cannot hear you, or see your living form, yet throughout our villages your sermons are scattered. And I know of cases of conversion from them, more than I can tell you.' Another friend mentioned to me an instance of a clergy-man of the Church of England, a canon of a Cathedral, who frequently preaches the sermons on the Sabbath—whether in the Cathedral or not I cannot say, but I hope he does. Oh! who can tell when these things are printed what hearts they may reach, what good they may effect? Words that I spoke three weeks ago eyes are now perusing, while tears are gushing from them as they read! Glory be to God most high!"

The sermons have become one of the institutions of the church in both the Old and the New World. What should also be universally known is, that the preacher has virtually ministered to his church and congregation for nothing; that is to say, the income received has all been given away in furtherance of the Lord's work in many departments.

MR. SPURGEON'S BOOKS.

" It may be added that though the comments were the work of my health, the rest of the volume is the product of my sickness. When protracted illness and weakness laid me aside from daily preaching, I resorted to my pen as an available means of doing good. I would have preached had I been able, but as my Master denied me the privilege of thus serving Him, I gladly availed myself of the other method of bearing testimony for His name."—*The Treasury of David, Preface to Vol. I.*

" I prepared these figures and metaphors that they may serve as *feathers for arrows*, arrows of Gospel truth which I pray may be made sharp in the hearts of the King's enemies."—*Feathers for Arrows.*

" I have somewhat indulged the mirthful vein, but ever with so serious a purpose that I ask no forgiveness. Those who see a virtue in dulness have full permission to condemn, for a sufficient number will approve."—*John Ploughman's Pictures.*

IX

MR. SPURGEON'S BOOKS.

SOON after he came to London Mr. Spurgeon appeared before the world as an author ; and each successive year has so added to his works in this department that, inclusive of the magazine, nearly a hundred volumes have been sent out. If the reader will accept the paradox, Mr. Spurgeon has never written sermons, although during twenty years his sermons have been to him an exercise in writing. In one of those autobiographical articles with which he sometimes enriches the pages of *The Sword and the Trowel,* he says : " The earlier sermons, owing to my constant wanderings abroad, received scarcely any revision, and consequently they abound in colloquialisms and other offences, very venial in extempore discourse, but scarcely tolerable in print ; the latter specimens are more carefully corrected, and the work of revision has been a very useful exercise to me, supplying, in great measure, that training in correct language which is obtained by those who write their productions before they deliver them. The labour has been far greater than some suppose, and has usually occupied the best hours of Monday, and involved the burning of no inconsiderable portion of midnight oil. Feeling that I had a constituency well deserving my best efforts, I have never grudged the hours, though often the brain has been wearied, and the pleasure has hardened into a task."

After reading the above explanation we well understand how tongue and pen have worked together to redound to the advantage of both. As a young man Mr. Spurgeon did not entertain very enlarged views concerning the dignity of authorship, and his expectations in regard to the profits of a writer were of a very modest kind. He commenced by committing a mistake for which he paid dear. The copyright of *The Saint and His Saviour* which would have been cheap at £1,000, was sold for a twentieth part of that sum ; and the small honorarium was never supplemented by the fortunate publishers. That mistake has not been repeated ; and his literary works have, since that day, been sufficiently varied and numerous to represent the fruits of a busy literary life quite apart from the regular issue of the sermons. Hence it appears that a phenomenon is now seen in the printing and publishing world which it would be hard to parallel—extensive printing works in one part of the city, and a publishing house in another quarter, are in the main supplied with grist from the study of one man, and that man a Baptist minister, preaching what many call " narrow theology." Yet they who class the sermons among " narrow " productions will not forget that they are sown over a broader field than is the case with the discourses of any other preacher.

Though Mr. Spurgeon is continually suffering from the effects of over-work, the public is still exacting in its demands ; and to judge by the editions issued, readers eagerly welcome each successive offspring of the author's diligent application. Though *John Ploughman* is the Pastor's most popular character, *The Treasury of David* is his *magnum opus.* In the first he writes like one who can do taskwork well ; amid the green pastures and quiet waters of the Psalms he explores a congenial land where every advance reveals new beauties, and where labour yields a sweet reward.

The Treasury of David, just completed in seven octavo volumes, has the virtue of being the production of a writer who has been in love with the Psalms from his youth ; and, indeed, this enthusiasm for the subject was necessary, for the

work has been only completed after more than
twenty years of arduous labour.   The exposition
bespeaks its author throughout ; it abounds in
that epigrammatic wisdom which is a sure mark
of original genius.   Commentaries of olden times
—Manton's " long-metre edition of Psalm cxix."
being a well-known example—rather alarmed than
attracted inquisitive readers ; but after tasting
of Mr. Spurgeon's fare, a self-indulgent literary
epicure might desire to come again.   The book,
with its ample store of illustrations, gathered from
the entire field of literature, ought to have entertained Dr. Johnson on a journey even better than
Cocker's Arithmetic.   While it is a rich storehouse
for the use of professional men, another, seeking
relaxation from the wear and tear of commerce,
might make the book a companion on a summer
holiday.   What is it but the triumph of genius
when studies, hitherto supposed to be only
suitable for ministers and collegians, are made
attractive to general readers ?

Here and there a metrical version of a favourite
psalm is inserted to make an agreeable variation.
In another place scientific infidels are described
as men who " will not touch Him [Christ] with
the finger of faith ; but they will pluck at Him with
the finger of malice."   Sentences which would
serve as proverbs might be plentifully gathered.

It is also interesting to take note of the skill with which the illustrations are selected. Take the following on the opening verse of Psalm xcviii. :—

"A clergyman in the county of Tyrone had for some weeks observed a little ragged boy come every Sunday and place himself in the centre of the aisle, directly opposite the pulpit, where he seemed exceedingly attentive to the services. He was desirous of knowing who the child was, and for this purpose hastened out after the sermon several times, but never could see him, as he vanished the moment service was over, and no one knew whence he came or anything about him. At length the boy was missed from his usual situation in the church for some weeks. At this time a man called on the minister, and told him a person very ill was desirous of seeing him ; but added, 'I am really ashamed to ask you to go so far ; but it is a child of mine, and he refuses to have any one but you. He is altogether an extraordinary boy, and talks a great deal about things that I do not understand.' The clergyman promised to go, and went, though the rain poured down in torrents, and he had six miles of rugged mountain country to pass. On arriving where he was directed, he saw a most wretched cabin indeed and the man he had seen in the morning was

waiting at the door.   He was shown in, and
found the inside of the hovel as miserable as the
outside.   In a corner, on a little straw, he beheld
a person stretched out, whom he recognised as
the little boy who had so regularly attended his
church.   As he approached the wretched bed the
child raised himself up, and stretching forth his
arms said, ' *His own right hand and His holy arm
hath gotten Him the victory*,' and immediately he
expired."

The work on the Psalms entailed enormous
labour, not merely as a commentary, but on
account of the vast array of illustrative passages
which have been gathered from the great field of
the world's literature ; and it must at least be a
great consolation to Mr. Spurgeon and his assistants to see how thoroughly their work has been
appreciated by the public.   At the time of
writing, about 107,000 volumes have been sent out,
and this is of course a number far beyond the
circulation that any commentary on a single book
of the Bible has ever before commanded.

To persevere in a task through more than
twenty years, when the labour increases in difficulty
as it proceeds, is an example of industry not
often encountered ; but this is what Mr. Spurgeon
has done while completing his *Treasury of
David.*   The ancient classics of Greece and Italy

have been read for any dust of gold they might
contain ; so also have the Christian Fathers, the
English classics, and others, to mention the names
of which would only tend to the bewilderment of
the unlearned reader.

But Mr. Spurgeon is more than a commentator,
he is a many-sided genius,—that is, he can work
to advantage in various departments, and excel
in all.   In *The Treasury of David* he is the ripe
theologian ; in the character of *John Ploughman* he talks philosophy such as the common
people like to hear because they can understand ;
in his *History of the Tabernacle* he is a painstaking historian ; in *Lectures to My Students*
he is a more lively college professor than any
other member of that honourable fraternity with
whom I am acquainted.   It is worth a substantial
entrance fee to listen to one of these Friday
afternoon orations ; but those who cannot hear
should read the book.

In old times, when books were scarce, and good
teachers scarcer, a clever University lecturer would
attract auditors from foreign climes, who in after
life were wont to boast of early privileges.   It is
really surprising to think how the old schoolmen
killed time, and wasted their energies in battling
about barren topics, or in establishing their finely-
spun theories.   The popular mediæval professor,

17

with his host of determined disciples, was hardly
a less formidable opponent than we should now
find in a confident general who knew that
regiments of veterans were ready to give effect
to his orders. The shock of controversy often
troubled the outside world; but whether the
Realists or the Idealists held the field mattered
little to the vulgar crowd. Was it ever authori-
tatively decided whether a thousand angels could,
or could not dance upon the point of a finely-
sharpened needle? Philosophy was a dead letter,
because men worshipped intellect and learning for
their own sake, without caring anything about the
elevation of the benighted population. Students
spent their strength for nought, losing their way
in the mazes of casuistry, until nothing short of
the mighty awakening of the Reformation sufficed
to break their fatal dream.

Had Mr. Spurgeon flourished in mediæval days
he would have been renowned as a man of valour,
the Achilles of a school, and even now he is
scarcely less than this. No college professor ever
before gave lectures precisely similar to " Lectures
to My Students." The book is weighty and
piquant, serious as well as sparkling; many of its
philosophical saws gain force from their settings
of humour. In every sense it is a popular reading-
book; one not too light for grave scholars, nor of

that solid dryness which repels those who read for
amusement. Every page is racy, the wit is free
from ill-nature, and throughout there is a characteristic striving after practical results. Pretty
things are never said for their own sake; the
smallest apophthegm is aimed at a high mark
which is seldom missed. As college homilies
these lectures were not delivered with that professional frown which might seem to give weight
to their matter and dignity to the lecturer; they
were rather spoken with easy grace, and as we
read we seem to be looking on a beaming countenance which of itself may teach what is worth
even more than a college lesson. "Our reverend
tutor, Mr. Rogers, compares my Friday work to
the sharpening of the pin," we are told; "the
fashioning of the head, the straightening, the
laying on of the metal, and the polishing, have
been done during the week, and then the process
concludes with an effort to give point and sharp-
ness. To succeed in this the lecturer must not
be dull himself, nor demand any great effort from
his audience. I am as much at home with my
young brethren as in the bosom of my family,
and, therefore, speak without restraint."

Mr. Spurgeon lets his readers know who the
young aspirants are that constitute the Pastors'
College, and also who they are *not*. To those who

assert that he has set up a clerical factory, he
replies that he is rather a " parson killer." He is
ever doing work similar to "the duty which fell
to the lot of Cromwell's Triers." He does not
want men who are striving to do the best they
can for themselves in this world, and applications
are declined which come from those whose " main
object is an ambitious desire to shine among men."
Self-conceited geniuses are always kindly directed
elsewhere. Nor is it believed that the students
are generally characterised by "great feebleness
of mind," because applicants betraying a mental
weakness which is likely to be carried away by any
kind of doctrine are counselled to "keep in the
rear ranks," in company with other knights of "the
kid-gloved order." Another too numerous class,
who are not welcomed into the College, are "distinguished by enormous vehemence and zeal, and
a conspicuous absence of brains ; brethren who
would talk for ever and ever upon nothing, who
would stamp and thump the Bible, and get
nothing out of it at all ; earnest, awfully earnest,
mountains in labour of the most painful kind;
but nothing comes of it all, not even the *ridi-
culus mus*. There are zealots abroad who are not
capable of conceiving or uttering five consecutive
thoughts, whose capacity is most narrow, and their
conceit most broad ; and these can hammer, and

bawl, and rave, and tear, and rage, but the noise all arises from the hollowness of the drum." Of others the name is legion, whose natural defects would render them ludicrous in the eyes of a congregation. One applicant "had a sort of rotary action of the jaw," says Mr. Spurgeon. " I could not have looked at him while preaching without laughter, if all the gold of Tarshish had been my reward." Men who base their "call" on a hedged-up way are not encouraged, because "a man who would succeed as a preacher would probably do right well either as a grocer, or a lawyer, or anything else. A really valuable minister would have excelled at anything." Mr. Self-conceit cannot always see reason when his offer of self-sacrifice is declined. " Do you mean to say that because I have an unusual genius," asked one, in warm indignation, "and have produced in myself a gigantic mind, such as is rarely seen, I am refused admittance into your College ? "

Perhaps no volume sold for half-a-crown ever cost an author more trouble than *Commenting and Commentaries*. The student is directed to nearly fifteen hundred works, treating of separate parts of the Bible, or of the whole book. Like Lord Bacon, Mr. Spurgeon must see fruit come of his labour, or he is not satisfied. Such books are not written for money, nor for fame, for the sake of aiding those who have little money to spend in literature ; *e.g.* :—

" Here, however, is the difficulty ; students do not find it easy to choose which works to buy, and their slender stores are often wasted on books of a comparatively worthless kind. If I can save a poor man from spending his money for that which is not bread, or, by directing a brother to a good book, may enable him to dig deeper into the mines of truth, I shall be well repaid. For this purpose I have toiled, and read much, and passed under review some three or four thousand volumes. From these I have compiled my catalogue, reject- ing many, yet making a very varied selection. Though I have carefully used such judgment as I possess, I have, doubtless, made many errors ; I shall, certainly, find very few who will agree with me in all my criticisms, and some persons may be angry with my remarks. . . . He who finds fault will do well to execute the work in a better style ; only let him remember that he will have my heifer to plough with, and therefore ought, in all reason, to excel me."

It is taken for granted that persons who pur- chase the book value the assistance of Biblical expositors. " Of course you are not such wise- acres as to think you can expound Scripture without assistance from the works of divines and learned men, who have laboured before you in the field of exposition," the students are told. "If you are of that opinion, pray remain so, for you are not worth the trouble of conversion, and, like a little coterie who.think with you, would resent the attempt as an insult to your infallibility." His opinions on the leading commentators are not those of a man who has not taken the trouble to read their works for himself.

"First among the mighty for general usefulness, we are bound to mention the man whose name is a household word, MATTHEW HENRY. He is most pious and pithy, sound and sensible, suggestive and sober, terse and trustworthy. You will find him to be glittering with metaphors, rich in analogies, overflowing with illustrations, superabundant in reflections. . . . It is the poor man's commentary, the old Christian's companion, suitable to everybody, instructive to all. . . . Every minister ought to read Matthew Henry entirely and carefully through once at least. I should recommend you to get through it in the next twelve months after you leave college. Begin at the beginning, and resolve that you will traverse the goodly land from Dan to Beersheba. You will acquire a vast store of sermons if you read with your note-book close at hand ; and as for thoughts, they will swarm around you like twitter-

ing swallows around an old gable towards the
close of autumn."

John Calvin is " a prince among men."
Matthew Poole " is a very prudent and judicious
commentator." Trapp is recommended " to men
of discernment." Gill is a " master cinder-sifter
among the Targums, the Talmuds, the Mishna,
and the Gemara. . . . I have placed next to
Gill in my library Adam Clarke; but as I have no
desire to have my rest broken by wars among the
authors, I have placed Doddridge between them.
If the spirits of the two worthies could descend
to the earth in the same mood in which they
departed, no house would be able to hold them."
He goes on to say that the first money received
for services in London was exchanged for Scott's
Commentary ; but " for a minister's use Scott is
mere milk-and-water."

The *Metropolitan Tabernacle and Its Work*
would have been a work of more surpassing
interest had the author done what he thinks he
could not be expected to do—had he turned his
" pages into an autobiography." Mr. Spurgeon
will not, however, portray himself. He prefers to
see himself as others see him.

John Ploughman's Talk and *Pictures* are Mr.
Spurgeon's most popular books, if we judge of
popularity by the fact that 450,000 copies of the

two volumes have been sold. Then come *Morning by Morning* and *Evening by Evening*, the circulation of the one having reached 100,000, and the other 75,000. *Feathers for Arrows* and *Illustrations and Meditations* are illustrative manuals. *Flashes of Thought, Spurgeon's Gems*, and *Gleanings Among the Sheaves* are choice passages selected by other hands from an ample field. *Types and Emblems, Trumpet Calls to Christian Energy, The Present Truth, Storm Signals*, and *Farm Sermons* are supplementary volumes of discourses printed in crown octavo-form. There are several others I have not mentioned which command wide popularity. The shilling series extends to eleven volumes. *All of Grace* shows the plan of salvation ; while *The Clue of the Maze* is an antidote to the specious unbelief of the times. Nor ought *The Interpreter ; or, Scripture for Family Worship*, with its running comments and hymns, to be overlooked. As a handsome quarto volume, this book is frequently purchased for a wedding present.

The Pastor's printed books, including *The Sword and the Trowel*, thus comprise nearly one hundred volumes ; and form in themselves such a comprehensive library as was never before provided by one man.

In the meantime, the work of translating the

Pastor's works into European and even Oriental
languages still goes on. Mr. Spurgeon's own
portion of *The Treasury of David* is now being
rendered into Arabic, while *All of Grace* is being
rendered into German.

THE BOOK FUND.

" The room is small, and very poorly furnished, a tiny fire burns in the grate, for it is mid-winter ; but beyond this, there is an absence of all the suitable surroundings of a minister's study, and you can count the *books* upon your fingers. The pastor sits there with bowed head, and weary body, after a day of heavy work, and, shall I tell it ? of very scanty sustenance. A deep sense of responsibility is upon him, and he feels the weight of souls on his heart ; but in addition to this, special cares just now press upon him heavily ; troubles of church and building matters, questions as to ways and means, fightings without, and fears within, which vex and grieve him sorely. . . . Weary and faint, *he is very, very poor*, and almost overwhelmed by the difficulties of the way, he turns to the fire with his open Bible on his knee and sighs. Oh ! such a sigh. Will the angels hear it, I wonder, and come and minister to him, as they used to do to their sorrowful Lord ? Perhaps so, but his Heavenly Father has also prepared an earthly solace, and the answer to his cry is even now at the door. The bell rings, and a large parcel is left ' For the Pastor,' and is taken at once to his room. In a moment he knows that relief has come, he knows the superscription, and divines the contents ; in his joy he almost caresses the package ; then, with trembling fingers, he cuts the string, and spreads the treasures out before the Lord. Yes, literally ' before the Lord,' for now you see him kneeling by the side of the open parcel, thanking and blessing God for such opportune mercy, for such streams in the desert, such blossoming roses in the wilderness."—*Ten Years of my Life in the Service of the Book Fund*, 327-8.

X.

THE BOOK FUND.

AS a benefactor of poor ministers who are unable to buy necessary books, Mrs. Spurgeon has won a wide reputation ; and the beneficent work carried on is all the more remarkable because, in past years more especially, it was accomplished in spite of pain and weakness such as would have disabled anyone who could not have exemplified the heroism or endurance which sometimes seems to be peculiar to Christian women. The book distribution, which commenced in 1875, was originally undertaken on a very small scale ; and at first no one suspected that the giving away of a hundred copies of Mr. Spurgeon's *Lectures* would lead to the development of a comprehensive enterprise which would extend its influence not only throughout the British Isles, but also to the colonies. In her recently published work, *Ten Years of my Life in the Service of the Book Fund*, Mrs. Spurgeon thus explains how the enterprise originated, which, through the goodness of God, has often proved a solace as well as a labour to the person chiefly concerned :—

"It was in the summer of the year 1875 that my dear husband completed and published the first volume of his *Lectures to My Students*. Reading one of the proof copies, I became so enamoured of the book that when the dear author asked, 'Well, how do you like it?' I answered with a full heart, 'I wish I could place it in the hands of every minister in England.' 'Then why not do so? *how much will you give?*' said my very practical spouse. . . . Then comes the wonderful part : I found the money ready and waiting! Upstairs in a little drawer were some carefully-hoarded crown-pieces, which, owing to some foolish fancy, I had been gathering for years whenever chance threw one in my way; these I now counted out, and found they made a sum *exactly* sufficient to pay for one hundred copies of the work! If a twinge of regret at parting from my cherished but unwieldy favourites passed over me, it was gone in an instant, and then they were given, freely and thankfully, to the Lord, and in that moment, though I knew it not, the Book Fund was inaugurated."

Since that auspicious day the general distribution has not fallen very far short of 90,000 volumes, while the recipients have numbered considerably over 12,000 indigent pastors, who certainly cannot purchase an adequate supply of books if they are not freely supplied to them. Can we estimate the encouragement thus afforded to men who are often wearied and cast down through difficulties and perplexities which are aggravated, if not actually created, by poverty?

Very naturally, perhaps, some persons have supposed that the Book Fund is for Baptists exclusively; but writing in the early part of 1880 in her own pleasant style, Mrs. Spurgeon described the thorough catholicity of her work:—

"A day or two since the good Earl of Shaftesbury paid us a visit, and on leaving he said to me, 'Well, how does the Baptist book-giving prosper?' 'Thank you, my lord,' I replied, 'the Book Fund prospers grandly, all the more that it is *not* a Baptist book-giving, but is free to all the Lord's ministering servants.' If the venerable Earl could have seen my day-book he would have found full confirmation of this assertion, for glancing down the long columns of recipients' names, one cannot but be struck with the constant repetition of the distinguishing titles of Church, Congregational, Presbyterian, Methodist, etc., and the comparatively infrequent recurrence of the word Baptist in the list. Thus, in these first four months of the year, I have already on my books the names of nearly four hundred ministers, who during that period have received grants from my Fund, and of this number just *one-fourth* are 'mine own people.' I am delighted to see that the longer record bears the names of fifty Church of England clergymen, and I believe I am justified in anticipating glorious results from the distribution among them of sound and scriptural doctrine. And if in some cases appreciation should lead to appropriation, and from many a stately pulpit in the land the Gospel should sound forth full and free through the sermons first delivered in the Metropolitan Tabernacle, shall aught but joy and thankfulness fill our hearts ? 'I confess,' wrote a vicar to me, 'that though I do not preach your husband's sermons *bodily*, I yet so assimiliate them into my own discourses that they are of the utmost value and blessing to me.' "

Of the general need of the work among ministers of all denominations there can hardly be two opinions. I was privileged to assist in the preparation of the first annual Report of the Fund for 1876, and I then described the need of the enterprise in these words :—

' The position of Nonconformist pastors in sparsely inhabited country districts is extremely difficult, and ought to command the sympathy and help of all their brethren. On account of their position appearances have to be studied, and much of their scanty means must thus be expended. Even their rustic audiences would hardly bear to see the pastor in a smock frock and his children barefooted."

The above applies in general terms to the need existing for more books in the studies of our poorer pastors ; and that the case is not put too strongly is proved by the fact that the individual examples brought to light by Mrs. Spurgeon more than prove what is said. Thus, for example, in 1880, three representative cases were given of the destitution which exists in the households of three pastors of the Baptist denomination.

" No. I. is a hard-working, painstaking pastor, preaching five times a week, holding large Bible-classes, writing, itinerating, and in every way doing his best for the people of his charge ; he is married, has three children, and accepts and manages to exist upon a meagre pittance of sixty-five pounds per annum, supplemented by a new year's gift, which usually comes to about ten or twelve pounds. . . .

" No. II. is in a still sadder plight. For twenty years his salary as a village pastor has never exceeded sixty pounds per annum, and, to use his own words, '*It has often been ten, and sometimes fifteen, pounds below that sum.*' This, with a wife afflicted for thirty years with complicated internal maladies, seeking aid from many physicians, and being nothing bettered but rather the worse, added to other domestic trials, and many deaths in the family, is enough, one would think, to crush all preaching out of a man! 'Few,' he says, 'save our Heavenly Father, know the privations and struggles which we have endured these twenty years.' . . .

"No. III. stands apart upon a pinnacle of special and exceptional sadness. . . . The husband is weak and ill from the lingering effects of a bronchial attack which prostrated him two years since, a young child is in a delicate and critical condition, the wife, though in fast-failing health has just become the mother of their *twelfth* child, all living save one, and *the last five are under five years of age!* Their income from all sources, salary, small business, and gifts from friends included . . . fifty-five pounds a year! Can respectable poverty know a lower depth than this?"

The cases of poverty in one denomination are quite in keeping with those found in another; and we have to bear in mind that in consequence of agricultural depression and other causes the people are suffering as well as the pastors. Thus, one who has to maintain a wife and children on a little over one hundred pounds a year bears emphatic testimony to what may now be witnessed in the country. " He says' he never before witnessed so much poverty and distress in his district; yet, at the same time, he speaks with holy enthusiasm of the trust in God and resignation to His will manifested by the suffering people. 'It is no easy work,' he writes, 'to live in a place like this, where one sees 'trouble' written on every face. I could not go into the houses of my people, and see shoeless feet and empty cupboards, without doing something to help them. Many must have gone to the poor-house, or have died without medical aid, if I had not paid the cost.'" What a commentary is such action as this on the words "Blessed is he that considereth the poor, the Lord will deliver him in the time of trouble." There are no helpers of the poor like those who are poor themselves.

The strongest testimony to the value of the work is seen in the letters of the pastors themselves who receive the books. In a manner that ordinary persons can hardly understand, the parcels of books have carried gladness into many a beclouded home, while they have stimulated many a flagging ministry.

" When I wrote for the fifth volume of Mr.

Spurgeon's *Treasury of David*," wrote a Congregational minister in 1880, " I felt that you
would place me under an obligation of lively
gratitude by acceding to my request ; but when,
instead of one volume, I am the fortunate recipient
of seven, and all of them of great interest and
utility, to congratulate myself and express my
thanks to you in a measure proportioned to your
bounty, is a task more easily undertaken than
adequately performed. . . ."

Another pastor of the same denomination,
also writing in 1880, says : " Accept my warmest
thanks for the books, and also for the kind
thoughtfulness which arranged for their reception
on *Saturday*. Having been worried and worked
over-much this week, and feeling very far from
well, I was in a state of physical exhaustion and
mental depression, which by no means augured
well for to-morrow, when your parcel arrived.
The very sight of it did me good, and when I
opened it and discovered its precious contents I
cannot tell you how many degrees better I felt
at once."

The clergy of the Establishment, including
even many of the High Church school, have
received gifts ; and from the acknowledgments,
written in their own characteristic way, we see
something of the poverty which abounds in the

Anglican communion on the one hand, while there is superabundant wealth on the other.

A curate in the north wrote : " I felt on the arrival of your parcel as if I must be so un-ministerial as to jump for joy. . . . As the volumes lie before me on my table, my heart is full, and words can but feebly express with what pleasure I subscribe myself," etc.

In 1881 we find that Mrs. Spurgeon had to entertain an exceptionally large number of applications from the pastors of the Established Church ; and the cry for books coming from that quarter was responded to with a liberality quite in keeping with the character of the Fund, but which none the less on that account surprised the recipients. " In some cases it may be quite possible that the volumes are sought for the scarcely admitted purpose of wholesale appropriation, but what then ? " remarks Mrs. Spurgeon. " Notwithstanding every way, whether in pretence or in truth, Christ is preached, and we therein do rejoice, and will rejoice. How many a young curate, with small ability but gracious spirit, might serve his Master well, and feed the flock of God with more convenient food, were he to cast aside his own manuscript, and preach boldly and bodily a sermon from the Tabernacle Pulpit. I am told this is very often done, and I can but

say, May God bless the doing of it." As regards
the business of appropriation, we find that one
parish " supply" preached Mr. Spurgeon's sermons for nine Sabbaths in the parish church,
greatly to the delight and edification of the
parishioners. Nor did the good man adopt what
some will think to have been his singular procedure without good reason ; for he frankly
confessed, " Mr. Spurgeon's sermons are the only
ones which can be really understood either by
myself or the congregation."

At first sight it might seem somewhat anoma-
lous when High Church and Ritualistic clergymen send in their applications for books ; but
Mrs. Spurgeon, nevertheless, regards the phenomenon with satisfaction, because, as a certain
member of the Church declared, the Baptist
Pastor's works more accurately represent the
doctrines of the Thirty-nine Articles than much
of what is preached in many of the churches.

One of the "Advanced" school in the Midlands,
who received a grant, had a vicar who had denounced Baptists as " abominable Dissenters" ;
but the great man was not above writing a recommendation to the Book Fund on behalf of his
curate. " Tell Mr. Spurgeon I shall highly
value his *Treasury* and *Sermons*, and hope
to reap much benefit from his *Lectures to*

Students" remarked the curate. " I never write, without a prayer for God's guidance and blessing, and I shall study these books, looking for the Divine enlightenment. I send you a view of my church—it holds about seven hundred people, and to-morrow I hope to assist in *five services* and preach twice." Another, who also confessed that he was "what is called a Ritualist," said on receiving his books, "I shall point to this present as an instance of kind Christian sympathy under-lying considerable difference of religious opinions." He then went on to rejoice that those who really loved their Lord had so much in common not-withstanding outward distinctions.

Among those clergymen who have written about their adventures with Mr. Spurgeon's ser-mons, however, the writer of the following should perhaps rank first in point of interest :—

"Having heard that you kindly assist poor ministers with books, permit me to state that I am an ordained priest of the Church of England ; and though prevented by age from holding any permanent curacy, I am engaged at a stipend of £30 per annum in two villages, and have to go some distance on Sundays, in different directions, for morning and evening service. On the second Sunday in Lent this year (1881), I was reading a text, when suddenly I remembered the Three

Thens (Isaiah vi. 1-8), by the Rev. C. H. Spurgeon, and gave it as a morning discourse at ———. I was afterwards asked by a district visitor what induced me to select so singular a text, and another hearer said she had never listened to anything like it before, while the majority of the people were so pleased, that during the nine Sundays I was there the church was full every afternoon."

Such are the recipients of the Fund at home ; but in some instances the books find their way to the Colonies and to French pastors on the Continent. One of the latter in writing to Mrs. Spurgeon said : " Now, more than ever, Protestant pastors have a great work to do in France. The people are tired of the clergy, while, on the other hand, infidels are trying to make way, and they boast of their science, comparing it with the too-well-known ignorance of the Romish priests." Since the Reformation won its triumphs, partly through the evangelical books which were vended by the colporteurs, who can help wishing that the second reformation, which alone can save the country from imminent peril, may be advanced by the Book Fund distribution ?

The words of cheer and of appreciation which come from the Colonies are similar to those which are so plentiful at home. " I need not say how the volumes will be prized and valued for their intrinsic merit," says one in Canada on the receipt of a grant, "the inspiration they will supply, the food they will give to mind and heart, and also for the sake of the author, whose dear and beloved form I see outlined before my mind's eye every day, and whose ringing voice I fancy I can hear across the three thousand miles of ocean. God grant that I may be able to catch more and more of that high-souled, consecrated enthusiasm which breathes through his writings like the fresh breeze of morning."

But although the distribution of books is the chief thing to be undertaken by Mrs. Spurgeon, she has extended her supplies to the wives and children of poor Pastors by means of the Pastors' Aid Fund. A small affair when compared with the other and main department of the work, the Aid Fund has still relieved a large number of the most deserving cases of pastors, their wives and children, whose chief cross in life is extreme poverty. Not only money, but clothes are given, so that all the members of a family are found rejoicing together.

Thus, as one recipient writes : " We are all very pleased with the share we have in the contents of the parcel. This is something for wife, children, and myself, and everything is so suitable and helpful. I scarcely know how I shall feel when I get on the nice warm clothes, and my wife says she will look as she once did, in her new dress."

Writing of this friend in 1881 Mrs. Spurgeon herself says: "He has been battling this long time with no small tempest of adversity and sorrow." The preacher himself added, "I feel the load removed which has burdened me so long, I see my precious books saved from dispersion, I see the faces of my wife and children lit up with joy, I seem to hear the congratulations of those comrades in the conflict who have always stood by me."

Scores of cases might be quoted to show the need of the work, and every one is representative of a need which is no less urgent than widespread. Thus one pastor's wife, who is called by Mrs. Spurgeon "One of the bravest little women I know," wrote in 1881: "I have been so very unwell all the winter, that our expenses have been unusually heavy, and I had put nothing by for the little boy's advent, so when he came we had no money in the house, and having to take our salary little by little, times being so bad with the people, we hardly ever seem to possess any."

Quite in keeping with this is the confession

of an Essex pastor, who about the same time wrote : " We never were so straitened as now ; my income fell off last year more than twenty-five per cent., and I assure you we have wanted the common necessaries of life, and I have come to my last pair of trousers. When I put the note into my wife's hand, she burst into tears, embraced me, and said, ' What a mercy God has raised up friends to be so kind and good to us ! ' "

When we ask, Who are they who help this work ? we find that they are as cosmopolitan as those who receive the benefit. In the early days of the enterprise the growth of the Fund was supposed to keep pace with a certain lemon-tree in the greenhouse at Clapham. It will be remembered how the Fund was commenced by the surrender of certain crown pieces which had been carefully saved ; and this example of self-sacrifice became so contagious that on a spring day in 1881 Mrs. Spurgeon wrote : " Four crown pieces, labelled ' Silver-blossoms for the dear lemon-tree,' were sent to-day by a beloved friend to cheer my heart and help forward my work." Of course the sender had a confession to make—" I have had them a long time lying by ; for my dear departed mother used to save them as a little present for me, and I never before could part with them ; but when I read how you began your good work, I felt I must devote them to the Lord in the same way, and they come to you in love and prayer."

On June 16th, 1880, this letter arrived: "Please find enclosed a post-office order for £2 1s. 6d., and a small slip of paper which will explain the use to which the money is to be put. It was directed to be sent to you by a Christian friend of mine, Mrs. D——, of Greenock, and was found in a drawer after her death. I may state that she had a struggle to support herself by her needle, and selling small furnishings, and was long in poor health, but her heart was in her Master's work, and she now receives her reward." The slip of paper contained a note in the widow's own handwriting, to the effect that all threepenny-pieces taken in the way of business were to be "dedicated to the Lord's work under the hand of Mrs. Spurgeon."

Thus, while some give of their abundance, there are others who still give even though poverty might well excuse their doing anything in the way of contributing to the wants of others. Some give money, but good books are of course as acceptable as cash, the only drawback to presents in kind being, that on some occasions certain donors, with more benevolence than sense,

or with a nicer perception of their own conve-
nience than of the character of Mrs. Spurgeon's
needs, have sent mere lumber instead of service-
able works. Take the following episode by way
of illustration :—

"Would that my record of 'presents' ended
with those which call forth my gratitude and
admiration. Alas! I have to renew my yearly
complaint that people in mistaken kindness *will*
send me the rubbish they know not how else
to get rid of. I remember saying . . . that I had
received nearly every sort of inappropriate and
unsuitable volume except a 'Cookery Book,' and
I congratulated myself that such an indignity had
not yet befallen my Fund. But I have now been
brought to that 'lowest depth;' for in one of
the unwelcome parcels forwarded to me lately
there are two musty old tomes which bear the
title of ' *The Complete Housewife, and Accomplished
Gentlewoman's Companion*, being a Collection of
upwards of seven hundred of the most approved
receipts for Cookery, and above three hundred
receipts of Medicine. London 1766.' After this,
I thought I might have borne anything ; but
to-day has brought me a still sharper experience,
and I feel constrained to exclaim against the
cruel kindness of people who thus so thought-
lessly trouble and burden me. I had received an

anonymous note bidding me expect the arrival of a case of books for my 'Clerical Library,' carriage paid as far as possible. With much anxiety I awaited the advent of the case, and when it made its appearance its size was so imposing that I did not grudge the *nine shillings I had to pay for its transit*, confidently hoping to find many choice treasures in its contents. Judge, then, my annoyance and my indignation on seeing when it was opened that, with the exception of a few well-bound books, of third-rate worth, the case was chiefly filled with old hymn-books, works by Unitarians, and books against believers' Baptism! Does it not seem cruel to mock my dear work thus, and give me a 'stone' for my poor ministers who are asking for 'bread' at my hands? How to get rid of the rubbish was now the question. 'Put the old lumber in the furnace,' said an excited helper in the unpacking. 'No,' said another, whose manifest annoyance somewhat solaced me; 'no, it would only choke up the flues—it is not fit even for that use.'"

Such is the work of the Book Fund. Mrs. Spurgeon has conferred benefit on the Church both far-reaching and lasting; and the pastors of all denominations have become her debtors.

REVIEWS IN " THE SWORD AND THE TROWEL."

"Our Magazine . . . will address itself to those faithful friends scattered everywhere ; who are our well-wishers and supporters in our work of faith and labour of love. . . . Our friends are so numerous as to be able to maintain a Magazine, and so earnest as to require one. Our monthly message will be a supplement to our weekly sermon, and will enable us to say many things which would be out of place in a discourse. It will inform the general Christian public of our movements, and show our sympathy with all that is good throughout the entire Church of God. . . . We do not pretend to be unsectarian, if by this be meant the absence of all distinctive principles, and a desire to please parties of all shades of opinion. We believe and therefore speak. We speak in love, but not in soft words and trimming sentences. We shall not court controversy, but we shall not shun it when the cause of God demands it. . . . We would sound the trumpet, and lead our comrades to the fight. We would ply the trowel with untiring hand for the building up of Jerusalem's dilapidated walls, and wield the sword with vigour and valour against the enemies of the truth."—*The Sword and the Trowel, January,* 1865.

XI.

REVIEWS IN "THE SWORD AND THE TROWEL."

AFTER he had laboured in London rather more than ten years, Mr. Spurgeon established a monthly organ of his own, the title of which may at first have seemed quaint or eccentric, but which has since become thoroughly familiar to lovers of good things throughout the British Isles. Not that this threepenny magazine has ever really enjoyed a popularity commensurate with its merits, although the circulation has always been large for a denominational magazine. From the first, one of its leading and most attractive features consisted in the Expositions of the Psalms, which commence in the first number, and which have since taken a more permanent form in *The Treasury of David*. The magazine also showed that from the first it would become an authority on books ; for the quality of the notices given proved that those who examined the works for the purpose of giving judgment really took the trouble to read what

19

they criticised. Of course all the notices were not written by Mr. Spurgeon, and the editor early protested against the habit of some publishers affixing his name to advertised extracts. At the same time, when anything unusually smart or witty was said, it did not require any very acute judge to say who was the author. In quoting a few extracts let us begin with the poets.

"How briskly the fire burns in the grate! Yes, the editor has received a fresh lot of poetry." Thus suggestively opens a notice of "A Poem," *alias* "Bones and Fiddles." "We wish the author had let verse alone, for we do not believe that he would be half so prosy in prose as he is in rhyme.'

The following appeared in 1882 :—

" *Verse and Verse. Rhymes for Dinner Times. Poem on a Boot Jack. Ode to a Poll Parrot. Meditations and Agitations*, etc. Tirem, Borem, and Co.

"The above titles are given in lieu of many others which have come before us. Our table groans with Cowpers and Tennysons in an embryonic condition. A San Francisco paper having been driven desperate by voluntary poetical contributions, sounds this note of warning :—'We don't know exactly how newspapers were conducted at that distant period, but during some recent excavations in Assyria a poem on *The*

Silver Moon was dug up. It was engraved on a
tile, and close beside it were lying a large battered
club and part of a human skull. You may draw
your own conclusions.' We are led to quote this
as a warning to the many small poets who send
books of verses for review. Happily in our case
no club is kept on the premises, and we are most
gentle in temper ; but really, we are tried up to
the boiling point by the poetic coals which are
heaped upon us. Still, Job is our patron saint, and
we are resolved to endure unto the end. If any
verse-maker does not find his poem, or her poem,
mentioned in these notices, it is because we do not
like to cause pain by saying what we think about
the precious compositions. Please do not write
to say that your poetry must have been overlooked ; for the fact is, we have looked it over,
and think it the wisest course to be silent.
Perhaps the work is too sublime, too elevated in
thought, too superb in diction, for our grovelling
taste. Pray think so, or think anything else, so
long as you are happy. For the most part these
minor poets are our affliction, and if they would
be so good as to take offence, and never send us
another specimen of their wares, we would bless
them in our heart of hearts."

More recently, a certain " Romaunt " called
forth this response : "No ; we cannot. If we

were condemned to a week's imprisonment, or to read this poem through, we should be weak enough to choose the latter ; but as we are not driven to that alternative, we will neither go to prison nor read this blank verse." On another occasion we come across the question, " Is there any rule for writing poetry? Yes. *Don't.* So has a wise editor settled the matter, and in ninety-nine cases out of a hundred the decision is not to be questioned.". Again, "A cynical old editor, who overheard an enthusiast remark that nature is full of poetry, snarled out, ' So is my waste-basket.' " Another editor commends to his contributors the example of Tennyson, who composes very slowly, and adds, " Never send in a poem to-day that can be sent in to-morrow. Perhaps there will be a fire before to-morrow." On another occasion amateur poets received this general advice from one who keenly felt that their work represented "one of the miseries of the editorial chair." " We recommend all poets, good or bad, to write carefully, correct seventy-two times, keep the manuscript ninety-nine years, and give orders for it to be buried in their coffins with them. We only except our personal friends, and any others who read this magazine regularly : they have our plenary indulgence to write as much as ever they please and send it on to us, enclosing a guinea with each line."

In one case, wherein a second copy had been sent, the author fearing that the first had been overlooked, the unhappy editor remarked, " The volume is altogether beyond our reach. If we receive a dozen copies of it we are afraid we shall still gaze upon the work with wondering awe, but shall never be able to see wherein it is superior to Milton."

At the end of 1874 this timely manifesto appeared : " Poetry again ! This grunt rose as naturally to our lips as the words ' Cold mutton again!' to the hungry husband who had looked for better fare. The cross and burden of our reviewing lies in the poetical department ; we can never please the authors, and the authors do not often please us. Why do they print ? It cannot be for profit, their minds are far above so base a consideration. It must be from the notion that they bestow pleasure, and we can assure them that they are greatly mistaken. . . . It is the books the big books *to be reviewed*, that we are sore about, books of which we have two, three, four copies sent because we have forgotten to review them ; books we wish we could forget, and which one never means to say anything about for fear our memory should be cruel enough to remind us of them."

One of the minor brotherhood who had the

temerity to send in his production "Just after Christmas too !" was asked, "What does he want with Philetos and Zön, with two dots over the ' o ' ? What is the whole business about ? Why did not the author put it in prose, and then we should have known all about it in a reasonable space of time ? It seems that he sat on a bough and ' rocked his musings into drowsy rest,' and then dedicated them to Tennyson, ' the sweetest songbird of our native land.' "

Of course there is occasionally something to commend even in the work of minor poets, and when real merit is discovered it is cordially recognised. Many examples might be quoted were it needful to do so.

Mr. Spurgeon has never disguised the fact that he does not greatly care for tales ; he seldom reads these himself, but at the same time he has given novelists plenty of wholesome advice. In the case of one historical novel, written by one who was supposed to rank as a popular author, it was remarked : " Here are power, beauty, pathos, philosophy, theology, and history all strangely mixed together, and the result, while flattering to the author's powers, is severely puzzling to the reader. Half the ability here displayed, if only the style could be made clear and transparent, would be far more effectual than it is now,

How we wish writers would not be too clever!
It would make them doubly interesting and
doubly popular if they could be understood by
ordinary folk."

Of another historical story about Gutenberg,
the inventor of printing, it is said, "The worst of
it is, one does not know how much is true and
how much is a mere tale ; and this is one of the
mischiefs of this sort of literature, that it diminishes
the distinction between fact and fancy, and is too
apt to make young people think little of sober
truth."

Sometimes the reviewer's patience is about as
sorely tried with the smaller fry in the realm of
fiction as with the persecutions of the minor poets.
We find it said of one, for example, " The wood-
cuts are so hideous that no story could survive
them, and certainly not so weak an affair as this.
With a new story and new pictures, like the boy's
knife with a new handle and a new blade, the
book might then be worth having." But we
suppose that even this was outdone by a certain
" grey-covered shilling'sworth of pietistic nonsense
about Christianity in general, and Methodism in
particular;" of which it is added, "If Wesleyanism
could be killed by fulsome flattery and idiotic
goodyism this would be its death-blow. But
there—no one could read the tale all through

and our wonder is that the compositors could set it up; but they are a long-suffering race." Again, of another we have this definite verdict, " This is the silliest book we have ever read. Perhaps this will induce some silly person to buy it."

The teetotal movement is frequently advocated by writers of fiction; and one of these is depicted as " an accumulation of horrors, enough to make one lay awake by nights and shiver with fright ; and yet no one of the horrors is in itself overdrawn or improbable. We should not like to be a drink-maker or a drink-seller and have this tale within ten miles of us. It has a mysterious hand like that in Belshazzar's dream, and writes awful things on the wall of the conscience."

Story-tellers are also taught that mere eccentricity is not a legitimate road to success, such for example as writing in a provincial dialect. " It is the thought a man cares for ; and to get that one can put up with Cornish, or Scotch, or Zummerzet ; but when the vein of gold no longer appears in the quartz, we cease to be enamoured of the rock. You may write in double-Dutch if you like, when you have something to say ; but when your matter is commonplace, you will never make it go by writing it in your country jargon."

The wearisome books from the reviewer's standpoint are legion, such, for example, as " A wordy book about words, the value of which may be summed up in few words." Of another of this class we learn that " the title is the most striking part of the book, but we warn our readers that the only reference to it is found on the title-page." Then it is added, " What a pity it is that good people should be silly enough to waste time and paper and ink in writing what could scarcely benefit any human being."

The reviewer's office is thus no sinecure, and it is especially trying when a dry and empty theological book calls for notice. " A very thoughtful book, no doubt, but who will ever read it ? " we find it asked of one of these. " Some conscientious reviewer may perhaps complete the task ; we with equal conscientiousness decline it. Sitting one day at the foot of a mountain at our ease, we advised all our friends to climb it, and awarded all sorts of praise to those who achieved the feat : so now, we say, ' Here is a grand book for you, my lads ; never mind its being dry ; just tackle it, and show your stamina.' ' Oh,' you say, ' read it yourself.' Not if we know it. We have other fish to fry." But perhaps even this was to be preferred to another—" Rubbish in rhyme, without any reason." Then hardly more reassuring is an elaborate work on misunderstood texts by one who gives sufficient evidence that she also misunderstands them. In one instance a General is found writing an exposition of the last book of the New Testament, but harder to be understood than the Revelation itself.

There are some authors who succeed only up to a certain point; and the following timely caution addressed to a certain writer can be well accepted by many others : " The style is clear, crisp, and attractive up to a certain point, and will be sure to be read ; but we are half-afraid it is too ' preachy.' Souls are wondrously shy things, and must be very wisely dealt with : the old-fashioned tract style of writing is scarcely likely to do much to-day."

Books which attempt to tell things beyond such as are revealed are always a mistake, and are not at all in accordance with Mr. Spurgeon's taste. Of one of the best known of these we read : " Time spent in examining this rubbish we greatly grudge. Dreamy, foolish nonsense, with a touch of something worse. Messrs. —— have brought out many curiosities ; this is certainly one of the oddest of them, and, we think, the most worthless."

The following relates to the Welsh and their preachers :—" Our brethren of the Principality are as good sermon-hearers as any people under heaven, and their ministers, encouraged by their enthusiastic appreciation, are urged on to excel in pulpit eloquence. Moreover, as their language is, according to their own judgment—and they ought to know—so heavenly, so divine, it is no great marvel that those who use it are able to produce extraordinary results. As we see it in print, we feel that our friends are right; it is an unearthly language and to us unutterable. Ll and a w, double l again, and a y, and then the rest of the alphabet shot down like a load of coals—what can this muddle mean? The man who can pronounce these jumbles of consonants must be a born orator."

The writers on prophecy are a somewhat numerous tribe, and are a source of annoyance to old-fashioned students of the Bible like Mr. Spurgeon. "The subject has been dragged in the mire so long that thoughtful men are slow to write on it." When some "Short Papers" appeared some years ago it was said, "The best thing about these 'Short Papers' is that they are *short.*"

Of a well-known magazine, mainly devoted to speculations in this department, and the editor of which was personally much respected, it was said: "Its present light is not equal to the production of a lunar rainbow, such as lovers of the old-fashioned gospel of covenant grace delight to look upon; in its prophetic moonshine, and short-punishment theorisings we see no rainbow, unless it be a lunar one."

Again, it is remarked on this subject : " That good paper and ink should be wasted in maunderings over vials and trumpets is bad enough, but that Christian men should be led to draw vain imaginings as to coming events from the grand Apocalyptic vision is grievous to the last degree. The imposture of those who foretold the end of the papacy in 1866 ought to have covered them with shame sufficient to have deterred all aspiring prophetlings, but it seems to have called forth another band of vaticinators, who set the date a little later, or, more wisely still, postpone it to the year 2000, by which time they expect to have spent their profits, and to have retired from the scene." One writer of mature age made out that the geological periods of creation had corresponding periods in redemption. Says the reviewer, however : " The only analogy we could see was between the book itself and the earth when it was without form and void, and darkness was upon the face of the deep." Twenty years ago the " wonders " that were to appear before the end of 1875 were terribly striking to lovers of the sensational in theology ; but when a well-known cleric narrated some of these in a separate publication his work was characterised as " Probably the

wildest of all the wild things which the present
prophetic mania has produced. This volume of
nonsense is adorned with pictures such as would
suit the outside of a travelling show, and its
matter will have great weight with the sort of
audience which gathered to see Katterfelto and
his black cats, Katterfelto with his hair on end
at his own wonders, wondering for his bread."

From all this it is pleasant to turn to what
is said about Puritans, with whom Mr. Spurgeon
is probably as familiar as any preacher in the
kingdom.

Nearly twenty years ago it was proposed to
reprint Caryl's two vast folios on the Book of Job,
the reading of which has for generations been
regarded as the best possible discipline in the
virtue for which the patriarch was famous. Mr.
Spurgeon does not think with the crowd on
Caryl, however. " Caryl is not tediously prolix,
as some imagine," we are assured ; " he is deep
but interesting. Truly he is a mountain, but the
sheep feed even to the summit."

Then what about Bunyan, imitations of whose
allegories still continue to appear ? " If you eat
honey you cannot taste the sugar in your tea ; if
you read John Bunyan you cannot enjoy any other
allegory. There is only one sun, and when you
look upon it you never think of mentioning candles

in the same hour." Some years ago the Vicar of Elstow published a capital book with the object of getting a stained-glass window put up in the parish church. Mr. Spurgeon confessed that he could not see " the congruity of the thing." It was asked, " Why not repair a Catholic chapel as a memorial of Martin Luther ? or the Baptist chapel at Elstow as a memorial of Charles II. ? . . . If John Bunyan's ghost walks the earth it will haunt the church until the stained-glass window is removed, if, indeed, it is ever placed."

The writings of Gurnal are said to be " peerless and priceless ; every line is full of wisdom ; every sentence is suggestive." Of " The Christian in Complete Armour" it is added: "The whole book has been preached over scores of times, and it is, in our judgment, the best thought-breeder in all our library." Again, Gurnal " is one of the greatest of the giants of the Puritan age. Many of our modern theological treatises are so devoid of real substance, that we are reminded of the chicken-broth which the sick husband returned to his wife, with the urgent request that she would coax the chicken to wade through it once more ; but when we turn to Gurnal, the old English roast beef loads the board."

" Rare John Trapp," the seventeenth century commentator, is called " our favourite author."

His work on the New Testament " is worth its weight in gold at the least, and sooner than not possess it we would throw in a diamond ring or two, if we possessed such things."

Many leading divines of the second half of the nineteenth century are noticed. More than twenty years ago the prophetical doctor, *alias The Times* Bee-Master, diversified his pulpit vagaries by publishing a book on Bee-keeping, in which he expressed a wish " that somebody would send Mr. Spurgeon a super of good honey" to sweeten his temper. " Why he should need to drag *us* in among his bees, we cannot tell, unless it be that our faithful rebukes of Anglican abominations have reminded him of his own unworthy silence on such matters, and he therefore attempts to drown the voice of his own conscience by finding fault with us." It is then added : " In spiritual things we greatly prefer salt to honey ; remembering that it is written, ' In all thine offerings, thou shalt offer salt ;' and again, ' Ye shall burn no leaven, nor any honey, in any offering of the Lord made by fire.' Salt, though sharp and penetrating, is the deadly foe of all corruption ; and honey, on the other hand, though sweet, is corruptible, soon ferments and turns sour. Fire speedily spoils the sweetest honey. We advise the doctor to use more salt in his public ministry."

The opinion given on Mr. H. W. Beecher's
Sermons, published in 1865, would, we believe,
hold good to-day : " He professedly deviates from
the old American standard of orthodoxy, and in
the same proportion, as we think, departs from
the truth. As an improvement upon the theology
of the Puritan fathers, his teaching will be rejected
by the best of men in this and in every subsequent
age. . . . Lessons of moral wisdom, of social en-
dearment, and of practical piety, may be gathered
from these sermons ; but for sound doctrine we
must look elsewhere. It is a lawful book if a
man use it lawfully."

Speaking of the late Thomas Binney in 1868
The Sword and the Trowel said : " He has ways
of his own of putting things which some in years
gone by have been frightened at, but we greatly
question whether any man after all was sounder
at heart towards the old-fashioned Gospel. In this
delightful volume—" From Seventeen to Thirty "
—he proves himself to be the greatest business
man in the ministry. He talks as if he had been
bound apprentice to Mr. Samuel Morley, had
worked his way into the warehouse, had become
a partner, and was now appointed by the court of
aldermen to see to the morals of the city appren-
tices. He ought to be an archbishop over this
nation of shopkeepers. . . . Set him among a

very spiritual audience of half-pay officers and wealthy spinsters, and he would be like a lion on a hearth-rug, but for where he is and for what he is, where is his equal ? "

The editor has no sympathy with those who devote too much attention to objectors while the multitude need the pure Gospel. When a work appeared, " Ingersoll Answered," Mr. Spurgeon said, " We neither care for Ingersoll nor the answer to him. There is enough to do in England with cutting up our own brambles ; nine out of ten of our people know nothing of this American briar, and there is no need they should." He said also to another author on a certain occasion : " Why need ' Essays and Reviews ' and Dr. Colenso be put up just to show how elegantly they can be knocked down ? Orthodox divines too often do the advertising for heretics, and turn bill-stickers to the devil. Why should they ? We are getting tired of ghost-hunting."

Thomas Cooper, the ex-Chartist, and ex-Secularist lecturer, but who since his conversion has done good service as a preacher, etc., has long been a favourite with Mr. Spurgeon. " It is no disgrace to Cooper, or to any other man, to have been a Chartist," it is said in the magazine for August 1878. " The Chartists only lived a little before their time, all the points of their terrible

20

Charter having at length been granted, in effect, if
not in letter ; and there was nothing unrighteous
or revolutionary in their demands. It was a far
grander thing to have our mechanics caring for
politics than to see them fighting for a double
allowance of beer and a short spell of work. The
modern agitator is a poor being compared with
his predecessor of forty years ago. By so much
as thinking is better than boozing, the discontented
artizan of Thomas Cooper's early days was
superior to the man on strike of the present
period."

Some years ago certain books by Francis
Jacox were popular. " Mr. Jacox appears to have
read through the Bodleian and all other collec-
tions of books ; he does not talk like a book, but
like the British Museum library. . . . We do not
know any books in modern times at all like
Mr. Jacox's ; they are unique ; in fact, they are
curiosities of literature. . . . The man must be a
cyclopædia ; we expect to come across him one
day, and to find him bound in cloth, lettered.
He ought to be in several volumes, but we
suppose they are bound up in one thick royal
octavo, and contain more matter than a hundred volumes of Dr. Going or Dr. Septimus
Losequick."

In 1883 the Rev J. De Kewer Williams

published his lecture on " The City Mottoes, and
Other Wise Saws." This was said to be " a clever
talk by a witty man, who is withal as wise as he
is facetious. We spent a very pleasant hour in
listening to a reading of this telling lecture : it
was under the palmtrees at Cannes, but we forgot
our surroundings, and thought we were in the
dear old city of. Gog and Magog and Fog, with
Mr. De Kewer Williams for our pedagogue."

In 1880 reference occurs to a once popular
"History of the Jews ":—" Milman's is an elaborate
work, but it seems to us to cut down the glorious
Old Testament narrative to the dimensions of
an Eastern romance. There is not much real
breadth in these Broad Church writers : they can
hardly tolerate a miracle."

When " Julius Cæsar " appeared in 1865, *The
Sword and the Trowel* contained a characteristic
notice, *e.g.*:—" This great work is beyond doubt
a most valuable contribution to history, and an
honour to the pen of its imperial author. It will
not disappoint the high expectations which its
announcement excited. It is written with one
object, and works towards its intended end most
cleverly. Napoleon III. is the preacher, Cæsar
is the text to be spiritualized ; the excellences of
imperialism are the subjects of the homily, and
glory be unto my immortal uncle is the conclusion."

Children's books have always demanded a large
share of attention ; and by his notices of these
Mr. Spurgeon has shown how greatly he is in
sympathy with the little ones. Sometimes he
seems to be so enchanted with what is provided
for juvenile readers that he wishes he were once
more in a jacket himself, so that he could more
legitimately enjoy the literary dainties peculiar to
the present age. Then take this example of the
reviews—a notice of a work on geography which
appeared in 1880:—" Happy young England to
be taught thus pleasantly ! One while the tree of
knowledge bore thorns and crabs, but now it is
a dainty tree, beflowered as with golden lilies
of pleasure, and befruited with rosiest apples of
delight. *Geography*—have we really been taking
in a whole jar of that verjuice ? Yes, and we
thought we were out a-gipsying, roaming from
town to town, o'er hill and dale. Ah me ! This
is not the geography which made our little head
ache, and caused school to be a torture both to
the teacher and the taught."

We will close this chapter with a few mis-
cellaneous references illustrative of the wit and
wisdom on other every-day topics which is continually enriching the pages of *The Sword and
the Trowel* in the review department.

When many church-members are apparently

asking themselves how far they can go in conformity to the world, the following notice of Anna Warner's "Tired Christians," which appeared in 1882, will show what kind of sentiments Mr. Spurgeon holds on this subject :—" Just our mind with regard to dancing, theatre-going, and the like. Well does our authoress confess her difficulty in writing about amusements for Christians, since no such word as amusement, recreation, game, or pastime can be found in the Scriptures. No : in the sacred book we read that time is short, and we are bidden to redeem it, but never taught how to waste it. . . . Tired Christians will find frivolous amusement a poor means of rest ; we fear that many are more wearied by their play than by their work, and are more likely to be jaded by dissipation than by devotion."

What is the relationship between work and genius ? The answer occurs in a notice of Mr. H. Curwen's " Plodding On," published in 1879 : " By the way, it would be a gross error if men imagined that men of genius do not work. To our mind, genius generally means that a man has a tendency and an aptitude for double toil in a certain direction, and hence he prospers in it. A genius for hard work is the only genius we believe in. We once knew a fellow who was called a *genius*, and boasted that he could make his fortune in a year: the last time we heard of him he could not make a personal call to borrow five shillings because his uncle detained his coat and waistcoat. We shall not advertise for him if we never hear of him again."

What is Spiritualism? The question was answered in Mr. Pridham's "Spirits Tried," published in 1874. In a notice of that work we read :—" We had aforetime considered Spiritualism to be a mere humbug, to be best assailed by ridicule, and such we still believe it to be in most cases; but Mr. Pridham's work puts a more serious face upon the business, and certainly makes us think that the devil has a good deal more to do with it than we imagined. We gave him credit for more sense; he is certainly a greater fool than we took him to be. We always had the lowest possible opinion of him morally, but we thought he could not come down so low as to be in league with idiotic spiritualists. He is certainly a deal meaner than when Milton wrote about him."

Writers who are too florid are not generally admired, especially in *The Sword and the Trowel;* so that in order to catch the editor's attention, and to command his approbation, it is not well to be " one of those who would go into raptures over a broomstick, and praise the picturesque beauty of a dust-heap." Nor in general does plagiarism meet with anything short of the severest condemnation. I will close these extracts with a description of the treatment accorded to a book whose author was detected in stealing other people's wares. The work in question was published some years ago, and related to the pulpit, its occupants, its literature, etc. *" Notes on reading this volume :*—Received it with great pleasure, liking the subject and respecting the publisher, and also the author. . . . Reached page 12, and smelt a strong smell of Roman candles while reading remarks on baptismal regeneration, fonts, and altars. Passed on, and began to sniff again, for there was a remarkable odour of abounding plagiarism. Remembered to have heard Mr. Paxton Hood's lectures to our young men, now published as ' Lamps, Pitchers, and Trumpets ' ; marked the same extracts, often beginning and ending with the same word, and with the same headings. Pitched the book to the other end of the room, and despite a few interesting novelties could not bring our soul to do other than cry out, ' Dead robbery ! ' Picked up the book with its back broken, and muttered, ' Served it right.' "

Every month the pages of Mr. Spurgeon's

magazine devoted to reviews thus contain a great fund of instruction as well as of entertainment. In a word, Mr. Spurgeon, who is the most celebrated preacher of this age, has also made his mark as a reviewer of new books. If we desire to see how he can deal with old ones we have only to consult his *Commenting and Commentaries.*

Printed by Hazell, Watson, & Viney, Ld., London and Aylesbury.

Date Due